From Physicist to Priest

John Polkinghorne in academic gown at
Queens' College, Cambridge

FROM PHYSICIST
TO PRIEST

An Autobiography

John Polkinghorne

First published in Great Britain in 2007

Society for Promoting Christian Knowledge
36 Causton Street
London SW1P 4ST

British Library Cataloguing-in-Publication Data
A catalogue record for this book is available from the British Library.

ISBN: 978–0–281–05915–7

1 3 5 7 9 10 8 6 4 2

Produced on paper from sustainable forests

Typeset by Kenneth Burnley, Wirral, Cheshire
Printed in Great Britain by Antony Rowe CPI

Contents

———⟶•⟵———

To Ruth and the family

Preface

It may seem a pretty presumptuous act for someone who is not a politician, or a sportsperson, or a media star, to write an autobiography. However, it would be a mistake to suppose that only celebrities have lives of possible interest to others. Most of us are low-profile people and we surely have some concern for others of similar status to ourselves. I am a scientist-theologian, someone who is both a physicist and a priest – a statement that sometimes arouses the kind of curiosity or suspicion that might follow the claim to be a vegetarian butcher. In our society today, many people seem to fall in with an unthinking and erroneous belief that science and religion are somehow opposed to each other and that the only honest thing to do is choose one side or the other. I strongly disagree, believing that the binocular vision provided by combining these two great human quests for truth is something that is necessary if we are to form an adequate view of the richness of reality.

My life has been varied. It has included long spells living the privileged life of a Cambridge don, an experience that afforded me much opportunity for the exploration of truth pursued in the gracious and historic setting of a College community. It has also included being a curate in a working-class area of a big city, and life as the vicar of a country parish in Kent. Throughout my life I have sought to take with equal seriousness the insights of science into the nature and history of the universe, and the deeper insights of the Christian faith into God's nature and purposes as made known in the life, death and resurrection of Jesus Christ. I have had the privilege of talking to many people about these matters, and writing a number of books, by means of which I have tried to share something of what I understand about the richness of the reality within which we live.

It is this variety of experience and insight that has come my way that emboldens me to write an account of how my life took me from being a physicist to becoming a priest. Now in my seventies, I look back on my life with gratitude for all that I have been given, and I want to share something of that with others.

John Polkinghorne

Acknowledgements

———➤◦◄———

I thank the editorial staff of SPCK for their help in preparing the manuscript for press. In particular I am most grateful to Simon Kingston for his encouragement to write the book, his valuable comments on the text, and his help in selecting the photographs.

It will be clear to any reader how much I owe to my family, and to my wife Ruth in particular. It is with heart-felt gratitude that I dedicate the book to them.

John Polkinghorne

1

Beginnings

Polkinghorne is a Cornish name, said to mean 'chief of the iron pit' in the ancient Celtic language of that region of Britain (though others say 'the pool of the iron chief', but I prefer the more romantic version). The Cornish are part of a Celtic fringe formed by their having been confined to the furthest west of Britain by the invading Anglo-Saxons. Their language, which has not been spoken as a living tongue since the eighteenth century, is akin to Welsh to the north and Breton to the south. Cornish people think of themselves as different from the ordinary English and, even today, when they cross the River Tamar into Devon they can say that they are 'going into England'. By the time I came on the scene my family had got as far east as Somerset, but my father had been born in Cornwall and, as far as we know, so had all his forebears. Therefore, I think of myself with some pride as being Cornish – one of the tribe of 'cousin Jacks', as Cornish people say.

My father George was the second child of the 11 children born to my grandparents, Richard and Beatrice. All were boys except the last, my aunt Bel. It is said that when my grandmother was told that at last she had a girl, she replied that she would as lief have had another son. The story is believable, since she was a strong-minded woman of decided opinions freely expressed, as various family stories record. One concerns the fact that some of the boys kept pigeons, with the inevitable result of mess around the place. One day after returning from school,

1

my father and his brothers enjoyed a particularly delicious pie for supper. 'What was in that, Mother?', they enquired. 'Your pigeons,' she replied.

Grandfather Richard was a stonemason, who helped to build Bodmin Gaol and Truro Cathedral. The family lived in the hamlet of Egloshayle, near Wadebridge, and Richard kept a cow and a pig to help to feed them all. My father and his siblings went to a village school, often taking with them a Cornish pasty that they would eat for lunch after it had been warmed up by the local baker. The village schoolmaster thought that Father was the cleverest boy he had ever taught, but the nearest grammar school was in Bodmin, and the train fare that would have been involved had Father moved on to become a pupil there, was beyond the family's financial capacity. Consequently, like his brothers, he left school at 14. My grandmother insisted that each of her sons should take up some stable form of occupation that had prospects for the future. In Father's case this led to his joining the Post Office, in which he had a good career, eventually becoming a Head Postmaster. Several of his brothers broke away when they had completed their various apprenticeships, in order to try their hands at chicken farming. In all cases this did not succeed, and they were then glad that they had some more reliable kind of job to which they could return.

Almost inevitably, my grandmother came to quarrel with her daughters-in-law. In my family's case, this happened during a visit to Cornwall when my elder brother Peter was about 18 months old. My mother Dorothy was feeding him a boiled egg at breakfast, to which she had added some salt. 'No child of that age should have salt,' my grandmother said. My father then got up and said, 'Mother, I see that you and Dorrie are not going to get on,' and they left that day, never to return as a family, although Father himself visited his parents from time to time.

This incident is one of those stories from the past to which I cannot help my thoughts returning. My father was a very gentle and mild-mannered man, so that his words and action had an altogether uncharacteristic sharpness. Clearly the event must have been the culmination of a long process of friction between the generations. One result was that I never came to know my Cornish grandparents, something that remains a matter of real regret to me.

The Polkinghornes were an independent-minded sort of people, small tradesmen who felt indebted to no one. My mother Dorothy's family were quite different. Her father Thomas Charlton was a head groom and his wife Harriet had been a lady's maid before her marriage. Grandpa was a very skilled horseman, both as a trainer and as a rider of hunters and showjumpers, winning many prizes in competitions at the shows. Had he lived 50 years later, when showjumping had become a popular television entertainment, he might well have become well known and well off. As it was, Grandpa simply worked for aristocratic employers whom he respected, and who respected him for the skills that he possessed. Life 'in service' with a good family involved a degree of deference, but in a manner that was in no way demeaning, and my grandfather was one of the happiest and most fulfilled people I have known. His last employer, Mr Cooper, had a horse, Snowy, that Grandpa rode with great success, winning prizes at the big shows such as the White City. The horse was eventually painted by 'a notable RA', as Grandpa told me, and I am proud to possess the sketch that the artist made on a visit to the stables, before returning to his studio in London to paint the full portrait.

As part of his groom's duties, my grandfather rode regularly to hounds as a second horseman, not tiring the horse in the course of the morning's riding so that, when he and his employer changed mounts at lunchtime, the animal was still relatively fresh for the exertions of the afternoon. Grandpa had a deep knowledge of animals and respect for them, whether they were horses or hounds, or the foxes that they chased. I have often thought of him during recent controversies in Britain about fox-hunting. Personally, I believe that our human relationship with nature can properly include an adversarial element, of course exercised in as humane a fashion as possible. Had I been an MP I would not have voted for banning hunting with hounds.

I was born in 1930 in Weston-super-Mare, a seaside resort on the Bristol Channel. In between my brother Peter and myself, my parents had had a daughter, Ann, who sadly died aged six months, after an unsuccessful operation to relieve an intestinal blockage. There had been some complications in the pregnancy and the doctors had told my mother that she should not have another child. However, she was bold enough to ignore their advice and fortunately I was born without any difficulties for her during the pregnancy. The birth took place in the newly opened Weston-super-Mare hospital (indeed, I have been told that I was the first baby born there), a fitting place since my father had been active in raising funds from his colleagues in the Post Office to help finance its building. Just before my fifth birthday we moved to Street, a large manufacturing village in Somerset where Clark's shoes are made. My father had become the local Postmaster.

I started my education at the local primary school. It had a fine modern building and no doubt it was a good school, but I got off to rather a mixed start. From the beginning I was very good at sums, scorning the assistance of counting shells as an aid to addition, but I did not make good progress in learning to read. Mother got anxious about this and decided that something must be done. She had a friend, Mrs MacAra, who was a Froebel-trained teacher and who was educating at home her own son, also a John and about my age. It was arranged that I should join him, and for about a couple of years this is what happened, with great benefit to me. Soon I was reading fluently and voraciously, a habit that has remained life-long.

I am very grateful to my parents for all that they gave me, but of course no home is perfect, a truth seen perhaps particularly in retrospect. We were lower-middle-class people with a concern for respectability. In our lives there were various invisible barriers enclosing acceptable behaviour, never manifestly spelt out but clearly understood all the same. As I grew older and into my teenage years, some of these unspoken rules became burdensome, particularly an implicit code that one had to be very careful about any friendship with girls. I recall thinking that it would have been nice to have asked a particular girl in my class to accompany me to the Saturday morning children's show at the local cinema, but I felt that this would not be a proposal welcomed at home

Aged 2, with toy dog

and so I did nothing about it. It is quite possible that I was over-sensitive about the matter, but I was a very biddable and well-behaved boy, for whom the mildest form of rebellion would have been unthinkable. My brother Peter was quite different, much more free and relaxed, in a way that gave my parents some degree of anxiety which, with hindsight, I believe to have been greatly exaggerated in their minds. Beneath his somewhat easy-going exterior, Peter was fundamentally a responsible person who would never thoughtlessly have got anyone into trouble.

This somewhat close home atmosphere was reinforced by my mother's personality. She could at times create around herself an air of possessing unusual gifts, for which the Polynesian word 'mana' comes to mind. 'I'm as good as a witch,' she would say after some clever guess about what was going on, and one was sometimes given the impression that she possessed remarkable abilities. I remember the Head Postmaster of Bridgwater, my father's immediate boss, coming to supper once at our home. Naturally Mother was anxious to exercise her certainly considerable cooking skills to the maximum effect. The main course was a veal and ham pie, with a hard-boiled egg perfectly centred in the middle. It was an achievement to be proud of, but in my youthful innocence I somehow gained the impression that this was a feat that few other people in the world would have been able to perform.

Nevertheless, in many ways Mother really was a remarkable woman. Outside the family she was much more relaxed in her dealings with people whose behaviour might have had dubious aspects than one might have expected her to be. They could talk to her about their lives and problems – this was true both for neighbours and for strangers on a train – and it seems to me that she was frequently able to be sensible and kind in listening to them and helping them. Mother had a great love of literature, particularly Charles Dickens, which she readily passed on to me. She also had good taste – learned partly, I believe, from acquaintance with the stately homes of my grandfather's employers – and in an age of country house sales before *Antiques Roadshow* raised public awareness of values, she was often able to buy nice objects at modest prices. We have a number of pieces of Staffordshire china and similar items, which I treasure both for their own sake and as mementoes of Mother.

My father, like his father before him, was a quiet sort of person. He had been a spare-time member of the Yeomanry before 1914, and when the Great War broke out he immediately volunteered for service overseas, not at that time a necessity for members of the Territorial Army. Being a Post Office employee, he was a fluent Morse operator and so he was transferred to the Royal Engineers, which at that time included the Army Signals. Incidentally, this may well have saved his life, for later when the Yeomanry were required to serve abroad, many of his former comrades were drowned when their troopship was torpedoed in the Channel. Father served in France throughout the war, mostly behind the lines at various headquarters signals units. It was a period of his life that he seldom spoke about, though he did sometimes recall having seen the primitive tanks of the day being moved up to the front for their first engagement in battle. After the war he met Mother, who also worked in the Post Office. At that time she was engaged to another man, but Father cheerfully said, 'All's fair in love and war', successfully wooed her, and they were married in 1920.

It is so difficult to imagine one's parents when they were young and every time I recall how Father pressed his suit against initial odds, I am amazed at his displaying such undaunted boldness.

My parents did not talk much to their children about religion, but it clearly mattered to both of them and we were a devout family, regular in our church attendance. I cannot recall a time when I was not in some real way a member of the worshipping and believing community of the Church. I absorbed Christianity through the pores, so to speak, perhaps to a greater degree than a more direct form of instruction would have conveyed. Going to church was helped by the fact that our local vicar, Richard Daunton-Fear, was an exceptionally interesting preacher, able to make Bible scenes and stories come alive, and I did not have any difficulty in listening to his sermons.

When I was about 7, my educational arrangements changed again. The Clarks all lived around Street, in the neighbourhood of their shoe business, and their families combined to run a small school, principally for their own children but with some select others also allowed to attend. I was one of these 'extras' at the Quaker school, as we called it, since it was next to the meeting house, also maintained by the Clarks who were all solidly Quakers in religion. The school took pupils between the ages of 7 and 11. It was always small in number (certainly fewer than 20), with just one gifted teacher, Miss Theobald. It provided a happy and effective education, conducted according to the scheme of the PNEU (the Parents' National Educational Union), whose stirring motto was 'I am, I can, I ought, I will'.

During my time at the Quaker school I had an experience that I can now see was a significant one. I was a clever little boy, my pieces of work continually gaining gold or silver stars that would then be affixed opposite my name on a notice board, making a growing line of achievement. One day, Miss Theobald said that she would do something different and give us a musical test. She played a series of pairs of notes on the piano and we were asked to write down whether the first or the second was the higher. I wrote down my answers and confidently handed them in, expecting another gold star. Not at all! Many of them were wrong. I was

'I am, I can, I ought, I will'
A happy schoolboy

taken aback, but not humiliated, by this salutary discovery of my limitations. Retrospectively I can see that it was a useful, and of course necessary, lesson to learn.

I love music and I greatly enjoy singing, but I know that my skills in this respect are distinctly modest. I have never learned to read music, and when for a while I was a parish clergyman, every time the organist changed the setting for the service I needed a lot of coaching from my musical wife Ruth to help me get to grips with a new set of notes. I was once on a visit to some nuns who are great friends of mine, acting for a week as their chaplain. It was the middle of August, and in their calendar, though not in mine, the fifteenth was the Feast of the Assumption. Reverend Mother asked me if I would sing Vespers on the Eve and on the Feast itself. After looking at the music which, as far as I could make out, looked pretty similar to that in an ordinary parish, I said I would have a go. It was only when we were about to start Vespers on the Eve that I remembered that there was no organ or other instrument in the chapel that could give me a note on which to begin, and so all our singing would necessarily be a cappella. Seized with anxiety, I began far too high. In a service nuns will follow you whatever you do, and we managed to stagger through, though my throat was rather sore at the end. The next evening, on the Feast itself, I was anxious not to make the same mistake again, with the result that we all ended up in some deep musical basement. I suppose the moral of this tale is that if you are a priest visiting a convent, take a tuning fork with you.

Back to education. Quaker school education ended when you were 10 or 11. The Clark children then went off to various Quaker boarding schools and I transferred to the small country grammar school, Elmhurst, that was located in Street. I remember my time there with great gratitude. Although a small school, it had some remarkable teachers who were truly dedicated to their profession. I particularly recall a characterful teacher of English, Miss Pugh. We read plays with her in class, including Shakespeare and Sheridan, an experience that significantly extended my appreciation of literature, although, apart from occasional trips to the pantomime at the Bristol Hippodrome, it would be some years still before I saw a live stage performance. We also had to learn poems by heart, but here I was less responsive and I am afraid that I have remained largely a prosaic person all my life. It has been suggested that for me maybe theoretical physics has filled the space that poetry might otherwise have occupied. There is a thrill in encountering a beautiful equation which I believe is a genuine, if rather specialized, form of aesthetic experience, but the cold clarity of mathematics appears quite far from the penumbra of multivalent allusion which I suppose to be an essential part of the mystery of poetry.

Soon after the beginning of the Second World War, my father was promoted to be Head Postmaster of Wells. Housing was difficult in wartime, so we stayed living in Street and Father travelled daily by bus to the office. My brother Peter had joined up in the Royal Air Force and trained as a pilot in Canada. He then returned to Britain and served with Coastal Command, flying missions over the North Atlantic. One day Father came home early from the office, looking strained and grey. He had received the telegram that we had all been dreading. Peter and the rest of the crew were missing. For a day or two we tried to cling to the slender hope that their plane might have been blown off course into neutral Ireland, for the night of their mission had been terribly stormy, but that was not to be the case.

*Older brother Peter as an
RAF sergeant-pilot*

Peter and I were very different characters. He was very social, a good pianist who was keen on jazz and popular music, someone who always seemed to have a rather glamorous-looking girlfriend somewhere around. There were nine years between us but we had become particular friends after he joined up. He was quite proud of my early scholastic achievements, calling me 'professor' in his letters, and in happier times we would have had many years of deepening relationship ahead of us. As it was, he did not live to see his twenty-second birthday. I was, of course, greatly saddened at the time of his death, but recovered in the way that 12-year-old boys do, not because they are heartless but because they live so much in the unfolding present. It was later that I came to sorrow again over the fact that I do not have a brother, nor my children an uncle. For my parents, the grief was much more prolonged, though self-contained. They had now lost two of their three children. Neither Mother nor Father ever explicitly imposed on me the burden of feeling that their hopes were now focused on me alone, but I came to realize that in a way this must be so. I was glad when I went to university and had some academic success, that I was in some degree vicariously fulfilling a possibility that had been denied to my father, despite those abilities that had been so evident to his village schoolmaster.

As the war began to draw to its end, my father was promoted to be Head

Postmaster of Ely. (He was known to be religiously observant and I rather think that the Post Office thought him particularly suitable for cathedral cities.) We moved there in 1945 and, since there was no boys' grammar school in the city itself, Father went to see the headmaster of Soham Grammar School, a few miles away. He took with him a letter about me from the headmaster of Elmhurst. When Stanley Stubbs read it, he generously advised Father to consider my going to the Perse School in Cambridge, admittedly further away but a place where I could be sure of having that great educational advantage, the company of unusually bright contemporaries. The Perse was a direct grant school, a kind of half-way house between state and private education, a partly subsidized institution that was thereby enabled to charge modest fees, tailored to parental ability to pay. Schools of this kind were the result of a typically English compromise that was prepared to straddle boundaries in the quest to be practically effective for the benefit of the common good. Unfortunately, later, when educational issues in Britain became subjects for ideological conflict and political commitment, the direct grant system was swept away – in my view, a regrettable loss of a flexible system that had served the country well.

Father accepted the advice he had been given and I became a pupil at the Perse where, after my first term, Mr Stubbs turned up as the new headmaster. I was a 'train boy', travelling to Cambridge from Ely every day on the not wholly reliable steam trains of the period. Such to-ing and fro-ing was a feasible, if occasionally tiring, arrangement. Inevitably it somewhat curtailed possibilities for my entering fully into the out-of-school activities that were a notable feature of life at the Perse. I did, however, manage to join the Perse Players, where eventually I rose to play the cameo role of Vincentio in a production of *The Taming of the Shrew*. The part of Petruchio in the same production was taken by Peter Hall, whose subsequent distinguished adult career as a theatrical director of international repute has made him the outstanding member of my Persean generation. I am able to boast that together we edited *The Pelican*, the school magazine.

When scientists are indulging in general chat, they sometimes get round to talking about how it was that their interest in science was first kindled.

Frequently the testimony will be that the torch was lit by the influence and inspiration of an outstanding schoolteacher. This was certainly the case for me. The master in question was Victor Sederman, who taught mathematics with distinct flair and a Welsh accent. In the fifth form, preparing for School Certificate (the exam later metamorphosed into GCSE), those of us who were good at maths were given the opportunity to do 'additional mathematics' as an extra subject. This would involve, among other things, being introduced to the differential and integral calculus. Mathematics is a funny sort of subject – when you do not understand a mathematical argument it seems impossibly difficult to penetrate, but as soon as you do understand it, it seems almost obvious and it is hard to see what the difficulty could have been. Maths is also an entrancing subject if you are lucky enough to have that kind of ability. Studying mathematics gives you an increasing sense of power, for this week you can solve an equation that would have been beyond you last week. I fell in love with mathematics, and Vic Sederman did all he could to foster the romance.

When it came to sixth-form work, it was almost inevitable that I should choose 'double maths' (pure and applied), together with physics, for the three subjects that I needed to study for Higher Certificate (the precursor of the A-levels of the present system). It seemed equally natural that I should begin to think about the possibility of going on to study mathematics at Cambridge University. (At that time nearly all Perseans going to the older universities chose Cambridge in preference to Oxford, a pattern that would change later, well after my time.) In the case of bright boys and girls at that period, the preferred route to Oxbridge was to take the Scholarship Examination in the hope of winning an award at one of the Colleges. One would normally do so following the taking of Higher Certificate and after a further term of special preparation in 'the third year sixth'. However, in mathematics you can make rather rapid progress (particularly if you have Mr Sederman helping and urging you on) and I decided to have a go after only four terms in the sixth.

The Colleges were divided up into groups that shared a common set of exam papers, and the awards that might be given came in three grades: Major Scholarships, Minor Scholarships and Exhibitions. Candidates had to decide on a group and then give a list of preferences for the awards that they were willing to accept within that group. At the Perse, it was the headmaster's role to advise candidates on the appropriate strategy of choice. Mr Stubbs recommended to me the group containing Trinity College (which, ever since the days of Isaac Newton, has been a hothouse of mathematical activity), but he also thought (no doubt partly with advantage to the school's reputation in mind) that a Major Scholarship, wherever it was held, was particularly desirable. Accordingly, my list started with a Major at Trinity, then went on to Majors at all the other Colleges in the group, then back to a Minor at Trinity, and so on, concluding with an Exhibition at the College deemed least prestigious in the group. The exams took place in December, and before you actually sat the papers, you had an interview with the don who would, if you were admitted, be your tutor (in the Cambridge system, the one who would be concerned with your general welfare, rather than with directing your specific academic study). In my case this was Walter Hamilton, a slightly lugubrious classics Fellow of Trinity. (He was said to have proposed to his wife with the words, 'Jane, Jane, how would you like to see my name on your tombstone?')

Mr Hamilton looked at my long list of preferences and said, 'You surely don't want to have a Major Scholarship at X, rather than a Minor Scholarship at Trinity, do you?' Biddable as ever, I said I supposed not. He there and then persuaded me to truncate the list by deleting all options except those involving Trinity and, as a compromise, one other College (Clare, I think). Afterwards, I felt a bit anxious about all this. What would Stanley Stubbs think? I felt even more anxious after the exams themselves. The questions were, of course, pretty hard and I had thought that one would be doing rather well if one could complete about half of those set in the time allowed. Listening to the conversation of other candidates, I heard people claiming to have achieved much greater success than that. I began to envisage a difficult interview with the headmaster at the beginning of next term, as I tried to explain that I had not even got an Exhibition at X because I had been persuaded to exclude that modest possibility. Just before Christmas, these anxieties

With Father at
Weston-super-Mare

were dispelled. I received a phone call from Mr Hamilton telling me that I had been awarded a Major Scholarship at Trinity. I was obviously very pleased, as were my parents, though it was part of our sense of family propriety that one must be careful not to show this too clearly to others. Any suspicion of being caught being 'uppish' about one's academic achievements would not at all have been the thing. A little later in life I would occasionally be irked by the way that Mother would enthuse over some friend's child having got a second-class degree at University Y, while she remained silently restrained about the sequence of firsts that I was then gaining at Cambridge.

Yet I always knew in my heart that my parents were actually very much gratified by the academic achievements of their son. It was scarcely possible for that sixth-former in the winter of 1947 to realize how many gifts would come to him from that initial propitious step of gaining a Scholarship at Trinity. I have been very fortunate in the places of my education – Mrs MacAra, the Quaker school, Elmhurst, the Perse, Trinity. I can say with the psalmist that, 'The lot is fallen unto me in a fair ground: yea, I have a goodly heritage' (Psalm 16.7, BCP).

2

Military Interlude

⟶•⟵

I left the Perse in the summer of 1948, just as my family moved to Grantham, in Lincolnshire, where my father was to hold his last Head Postmastership before retiring. I could not go straight on to university because I had to do my National Service. In fact I went into the Army almost immediately, well before my eighteenth birthday. At that time the period of service required was only a year, and so those of us who wanted to be free to go up to university in October 1949 were allowed to join up as early as possible in 1948 to get it over and done with. While I was in the Forces, the Berlin airlift crisis occurred, signifying a worsening in East–West relations, and the period of National Service was lengthened to 18 months. However, the authorities kindly agreed that people like myself, who had gone in under the old scheme, would be allowed out just before October 1949 so that we could go to university as planned. In consequence I only served about 14 months in the Army.

Military service started with three months basic training, which I did on Salisbury Plain with the Royal Hampshire Regiment (the 37th/67th of Foot). I had wanted to join the DCLI (the Duke of Cornwall's Light Infantry), in which at least two of my uncles had served, but the Army was not inclined to allow family sentiment to over-rule the tidiness of administrative arrangements. The train travelling down to Salisbury was crowded with ardent academic youth like myself, eager to get military service over as soon as possible. I could not find a seat and I had to stand in the guard's van, where I found myself in the company of another enlistee, Robin Turner, who turned out also to be a Scholar destined for Trinity in due course. Our barrack-room at Bulford Barracks was full of future undergraduates, together with a sprinkling of older men who had been allowed to take their degrees before doing National Service. Of course, having so much in common, we all got on very well with each other from the start. The young corporal in charge of us, observing our instant fraternity, asked after a few days, 'Was you all muckers before you came in?' We said we did not quite know what 'muckers' meant, but if it was friends, in fact we hadn't known each other beforehand. The source of our instantly getting on well together was that we had a lot in common, similar backgrounds and shared expectations for the future.

Basic training was strenuous: lots of drill and spit and polish (literally – it is a way to give boots an extra-special shine), daily physical training, all kinds of military exercises, from 'naming the parts' of the rifle and Bren gun to endless bayonet practice. The latter was a big thing with the Hampshires. The regiment had lost its 'Royal' in the First World War because of some disgraceful incident (rather glossed over in our instruction about regimental history), but it had regained it again in the Second World War by making a heroic number of bayonet charges on one day in the Western Desert. As a consequence we were continually having to advance on hanging sacks of straw, into which we plunged our bayonets while uttering (faintly) blood-curdling cries.

The Hampshires were 'Minden boys', one of the regiments that had taken part in the Battle of Minden in 1759. The advancing troops had marched through fields of roses on their way to encounter the French, and they had plucked the flowers and put them in their caps before going into battle. Consequently we too wore roses in our caps on the August anniversary of the battle.

The Hampshires were very keen on rifle shooting, as befits the infantry, and I discovered that I was a good shot, perhaps because in those days I had 20–20 vision. I was made a member of the regimental team for the competition for the Young Soldiers' Cup in 1948. On the designated day, teams of recruits from all the relevant regiments of the

British Army shot a competitive programme under the watchful eye of independent observers, there to see fair play. I had hoped to score a 'possible', but I had to be content with 19 out of 20. This was, nevertheless, a creditable score and my team-mates did likewise. At the end of the day we found that we had won the Cup! I have a bronze medal to confirm my part in this noble victory. It is inscribed on the back 'Pte Polkinghorne', with my Army number added. The latter is something one never forgets – you had to be able to repeat it instantly if challenged by anyone in authority, and I can do so as readily today as I had to be able to do almost 60 years ago.

It was not my intention to remain serving in the infantry. Like many educated young men doing their National Service, I had my eyes set on joining the Royal Army Education Corps as a Sergeant-Instructor. Not only did this seem to provide suitable occupation for the academically minded, but it was also said, by those who had already served, to provide one of the more agreeable ways to follow the military life. For me, however, there was a problem. The minimum educational requirement for joining the RAEC was to have passed Higher Certificate. I had taken the exams before joining up, but the results were not yet known. I suggested to the interviewing officer that being a Major Scholar of Trinity might be deemed equivalent to this relatively modest paper qualification. To my relief, the argument was accepted, but a friend of mine in the same intake (who later went on to be the headmaster of a famous public school) was not so lucky. He was a Minor Scholar of Trinity, but the Army did not think that was good enough. Brian had to go into the Service Corps.

For me, and those like me, the next posting after basic training was to a three-month course at the Army School of Education, located at Bodmin. Beautiful as Cornwall is in the summer, in the winter, which was approaching as our course began, it can be wet and windswept. It was. The course itself was interesting and it gave me the only formal teacher-training that I was to have in a life largely spent in institutions of higher education. As we progressed through the course, we were gradually promoted until, in the end, we had the three stripes of a sergeant.

There then followed the posting that was to occupy the rest of my brief military career.

I was sent to an Army Basic Trade Centre (ABTC) outside Malvern. Here young recruits were taught the basic skills that they would need in following a trade in either the Royal Engineers or REME (the Royal Electrical and Mechanical Engineers). My particular responsibility was to teach a refresher course in elementary mathematics to whose who were starting the course to become electrical fitters. This introduction lasted a fortnight, at the end of which I slid down the educational snake to start all over again with the next intake. This quick repetition was inevitably somewhat boring, but life was diversified a bit by various current-affairs programmes that we taught. I was also assigned to a special course intended to teach Warrant Officers and other senior NCOs (non-commissioned officers) the rudiments of algebra. I am not sure either how desirable or how successful this enterprise really was, but the seniority of the participants gave the course a certain cachet and, although some participants struggled, I found it an enjoyable experience to be their mathematical mentor.

In addition to our RAEC role, we Sergeant-Instructors had to take our share of regimental duties in the unit, such as being Orderly Sergeant from time to time, and being in charge of a barrack-room. As an 18-year-old, and young for my age, I did not find this easy. It was my responsibility to ensure that the soldiers were up and moving more or less at reveille (sounded on a bugle even in our not overly regimental unit) and that the hut we lived in was neat and tidy for the weekly inspection by one of the officers. The squaddies were about my age and they were certainly older in worldly ways than I was. I remember catching one of them stealing coal from the NAAFI one night to keep the hut stove going. One did one's best and three stripes helped, but it was not an altogether comfortable experience for someone whose upbringing had been rather sheltered to encounter these kinds of responsibilities for the first time.

Another task that came my way was easier to fulfil. Not being a dancing man myself (I suppose continuing caution with respect to the

In uniform as a sergeant-instructor, Royal Army Education Corps

opposite sex had something to do with this), on the occasion of regimental dances I found myself one of those entrusted with running the bar. It required a clear head, some arithmetic ability and, above all, honesty.

We were also required to do what we could for the sporting life of the unit. I have never had any real ability at any sport other than shooting, so the athletic aspect of Army life was somewhat problematic for me. In my last year at the Perse I had been a member of the West House rugby team which had been so full of talented players that we had won the House competition. Almost everyone else in the team was already loaded with sporting honours, but the event needed some mark of recognition and so I was given my House rugby colours. When I came to fill in my enlistment form, this was the only thing I could find to write in the large space allocated to recording sporting prowess (the academic section of the form was a different matter). At the ABTC, this gesture caught up with me and I found myself appointed vice-captain of the unit rugby team, playing as its hooker. In the event we had some enjoyable games, the toughest of which was against a local Army convalescent centre – not playing against the patients, of course, but a staff team with several super-fit physical training instructors in the side.

When the rugby season gave way to summer, I had to find something else to do. The Adjutant sent for me and told me that we had been sent some bicycles ('Like this,' he said, thrusting his hands down to indicate that they were serious machines with dropped handlebars). I was detailed – in partnership with another sergeant-instructor, Gerald Phizackerly, later to become an archdeacon – to form a cycle club (or rather, in the Army parlance that the Adjutant insisted on using, a 'club, cycle') that would be allowed out once a week for an afternoon ride. Our route had to be put on Part 1 Orders (the unit's scheme for the day) in case we were involved in an accident while off the premises, wandering around the lanes of Worcestershire. After a while, the Adjutant noticed that we seemed to be covering modest distances, which was indeed the case since our pace was leisurely and we always stopped somewhere for a cup of tea. It was suggested rather strongly that we ought to be going at least twice as far. Thereafter imaginatively extended routes appeared on Part 1 Orders, but somehow each week we found that the day's programme had, in practice, to be curtailed to encompass a more modest distance. I suppose I was learning how to become a little bit more worldly wise.

The officers and NCOs of our ABTC were a rather odd lot, since, apart from those of us engaged in various forms of technical instruction, they were drawn from regiments which had found they could manage without them. The provo-sergeant (the head policeman of the unit) was a fierce, battle-scarred little man, who readily inspired respect, not to say fear. One of the waiters in the sergeants' mess had been put on a charge by him for some offence, for which he was sentenced by the Colonel to a week confined to barracks. The waiter obviously felt that he had been unfairly treated and determined to make a dramatic gesture to register his opinion. I was sitting opposite the provo-sergeant at lunch in the mess that day when the waiter came in with the sergeant's pudding (to which, we learned afterwards, he had asked that extra custard be added). He flung it in the provo-sergeant's face, saying, 'Now I have done something worthy of punishment.' Dripping with custard, the sergeant rose to his feet and said to me, 'Johnny, put him inside.' I went into the kitchen to fetch the other waiter to act as an escort and marched the offender down to the guard room, where he was incarcerated while awaiting judgement. The Colonel avoided a court-martial and the erstwhile waiter (now demoted to the sanitary squad) was treated comparatively leniently. It was the most dramatic – one might even say violent – episode of my military career.

The Army kept its word about letting us out in time to go to university and I was demobbed just in time to go up to Trinity in October 1949. Like most of my academic contemporaries, I had not wanted to do National Service, seeing it as an unwelcome break in my education. Yet looking back on it afterwards, I came not to regret having spent a year in this way. It had given me experience of a very different slice of life from that which lay ahead in the next 30 years spent in the academic world. It also gave me something to have in common with all sorts of people with whom otherwise there might not have been much by way of a link. My generation still enjoys stories about the oddities of Service life.

3

Undergraduate

When I went up to Trinity in 1949, the system operating for being given accommodation was that rooms in College were allocated according to seniority. For most freshmen this meant that they would have to spend their first year living out, in one of the College's lodging houses in the town. However, if you were a Scholar you were part of the Foundation (the corporate designation of the College is 'The Master, Fellows and Scholars'), and so I benefited from the consequent right to have rooms in College from the start. I am glad to say that this system was changed long ago, and today all freshers will spend their first year in College, an arrangement that obviously greatly assists social integration into the community.

The 1949 intake into Trinity had an exceptionally large contingent of Scholars, since the vagaries of National Service had resulted in two cohorts arriving together, those from the year before mine having had to spend two years in the Forces, compared to our one. Among this more senior contingent was Michael Atiyah, the son of a Lebanese father and a Scottish mother, who was to prove to be the outstanding British mathematician of our generation, later becoming Master of Trinity and President of the Royal Society, as well as a Member of the Order of Merit. Michael became one of my closest friends and he was to be my best man when I got married. Another contemporary was James Mackay, who later abandoned maths for the law, eventually becoming Lord Chancellor. As a freshman reading maths at Trinity, I found myself in gifted company, and once again I was able to benefit from the stimulus of having many very bright contemporaries.

There were two speeds at which one could read for the Mathematical Tripos (as Cambridge calls its honours examination), the ordinary course and an accelerated course that omitted the first-year work (much of which scholarship candidates would have done at school) in order to get further into the subject during the three years of one's undergraduate career. Scholars were expected to go for the fast course, and that is what we did.

Teaching in Cambridge is organized on a dual system. The University provides the formal lecture classes, but it is the particular college that one belongs to which is responsible for providing supervisions, informal one-to-one or one-to-two weekly meetings at which you discuss solutions to a set of problems proposed by your supervisor, who in those days was usually one of the Fellows of the College. (The name 'supervisions' is specifically Cantabridgian; at Oxford they would be called 'tutorials'. The two universities are really very similar in many respects, but they like to maintain an air of difference by using contrasting nomenclature.) In my first term I was supervised in applied mathematics by Nicholas Kemmer, of whom more later. In my second term I was supervised in pure mathematics by a Russian émigré Fellow, Abram Samoilovitch Besicovitch. After one had gone through the set problems relating to the current courses, there was often some significant amount of time left to fill. Besicovitch would then produce a tatty scrap of paper on which was written some deceptively simple-looking but actually fiendishly difficult problem that he invited you to solve on the spot. As you sat there racking your brains, he would say in his Russian accent, 'I am surprised that so good a mathematician as you cannot solve so simple a little problem.' I never succeeded in doing so there and then, but of course you took the problem away to continue wrestling with it during the week, and quite often that resulted in a solution to be presented and assessed at the next supervision. It was a painful but very effective way of learning mathematical analysis.

I was now an adult civilian

As the years went by and one progressed through the Tripos, it became possible to specialize in one's studies, in the first instance by making some sort of preferential choice between pure mathematics and applied mathematics (that is to say, mathematics for its own sake, or mathematics for the sake of its being a tool for use in some other form of investigation, such as theoretical physics). Much as I loved maths itself, I had become particularly intrigued by the way in which it opened up an understanding of the patterns and processes of the physical world, and so I veered in the direction of applied mathematics. In my second year, when I took Part II of the Tripos, an examination in which those who get firsts are called 'Wranglers' (a venerable term, no doubt related to the days when examinations proceeded by disputation), I chose to concentrate largely on applied. Mathematical exams are particularly harrowing experiences, since you are required on the spot to do a bit of mildly original thinking in trying to solve problems that you will not have seen before. The mind needs to be really fresh to be able to cope with the challenge. Having this fact in mind, a bunch of Trinity maths

Scholars in my year decided that we would take a week off before the Tripos, letting our minds store up power, so to speak, rather than dissipating it in revision continued up to the last minute. Looking back on it now, I can see that it was rather a bold move, and one that obviously needed group commitment to the strategy in order to maintain nerve and dissuade individuals from reneging. We did it, and I am happy to report that we were all classified Wranglers when the class lists came out.

We Trinity maths scholars formed quite a close fraternity. One of our collective activities was occasionally giving a token present at the end of term to a lecturer whose performance we had particularly appreciated. Sometimes this took the form of a large bunch of flowers, and sometimes it was more enterprising – for example, we offered a lecturer in probability theory a spoof 'Boy's Box of Practical Probability', containing items such as a loaded die. This latter recipient clearly failed to recognize the genuinely positive character of the gesture, for, to our great disappointment, he refused to open the box on the spot, as if he feared it contained some unwelcome surprise.

By the time I had got to the third year and was preparing to take Part III of the Tripos, I was able to concentrate on topics related to quantum physics. The core course was given by Paul Dirac, the Lucasian Professor of Mathematics (Isaac Newton's old chair), who had been one of the founding figures of quantum theory and who was undoubtedly the greatest British theoretical physicist of the twentieth century. To learn quantum mechanics from Dirac was to get it all 'straight from the horse's mouth', as the saying goes. His style of lecturing was non-rhetorical and it was totally free from the slightest degree of emphasis on how he had made his own very important discoveries. Yet so profound was the material, and so closely structured was the argument, that one was carried along enthralled by the experience. Listening to the mathematical tale unfolded by Dirac was 'as satisfying and seemingly inevitable as the development of a Bach fugue'.

Being a Trinity undergraduate reading mathematics was a wonderful educational experience, but there was more to life in Cambridge than simply the pleasures of the mind. On my first Sunday there as a student,

I was taken to listen to the Freshers' Sermon in Holy Trinity Church, given under the auspices of the CICCU (the Cambridge Inter-Collegiate Christian Union). The preacher was the Revd L. F. E. Wilkinson and he took as his theme the story of Jesus' encounter in Jericho with the rascally tax-collector, Zacchaeus (Luke 19.1–11). The little man, who had to climb a tree in order to be able to catch sight of Christ over the heads of the crowd, had his life totally transformed by this meeting. Mr Wilkinson pointed out that Jesus was on his way to Jerusalem to die on the cross and that he would not pass that way again. If Zacchaeus had not acted when he did, he would have missed his opportunity. We were urged not to miss our opportunity, that very evening, to offer our lives to Christ for a similar transformation, and we were invited to come to the front of the church to signify that we had done so. A crowd did come forward, and I was among them. The words of the sermon had powerfully impressed me. I had continued my communicant Christian practice while in the Army, but in some other respects life away from home had got slacker – not very dramatically so, just things like some bad language and occasionally a pint or two more of beer than would have been prudent. I felt a call for a change and moved to the front of the church. That was the beginning of an association with the CICCU way of life that lasted throughout my undergraduate days and beyond. At the time I would have counted that evening as being the moment of my definite Christian conversion. It was certainly a moment of deeper commitment to faith in Christ and obedience to him, but I would now see it in terms of its being a significant further step in my Christian life, rather than its initiation, for I see that life as already having been begun in the setting of my Christian home.

As I look back at the evangelicalism of my CU days, I see much for which I am grateful to God: being led to a deeper personal commitment to Jesus Christ as Lord; encouragement to serious and sustained study of scripture; the establishment of a regular pattern of times of prayer. These gifts have stayed with me throughout my life. Yet there are other aspects of CU life for which I feel some sorrowful regret. In retrospect, I can see that there was a narrowness in the attitude that was inculcated, an encouragement of unnecessary inhibitions that fell short of the fullness and freedom of the Christian life. It wasn't just a case of not getting drunk, but of wondering whether a truly 'sound' person really ought to have that glass of sherry, or go with some regularity to such worldly activities as the cinema or the theatre. I had enough innate good sense not to give up such things altogether, but there was a certain bleakness that seemed to be expected of the faithful, which cast something of a shadow. I detect also there having been a degree of fearfulness about encounters with other points of view, including those of other Christian traditions, from whose shackles I am glad that eventually I found release. I am grateful that later experience has led me to value more than I did then, the grace of the sacramental life, which for many years has been a central stay of my Christian pilgrimage.

One of the absolutely important things that happened to me in my undergraduate days was meeting a student from Girton College, Ruth Martin, who was later to become my wife. I cannot now remember how we first met. It might have been through the CU, for Ruth was also a member, or it might have been through the Archimedeans (the university student mathematical society), for she too was reading maths, though on the ordinary course so that we never actually went to lectures together, or it might have been through a mutual friend. In those days, there were ten male undergraduates for every female undergraduate in Cambridge, so it seemed something of a feat to have acquired a girl-friend.

Friendship gradually developed into something warmer – I recall particularly one romantic summer evening during Long Vacation Term, lying in a punt as we listened to madrigals being sung on the river. There were plays to go to together and concerts to attend, in some of which Ruth would be playing. She came from a musical family in which her learning to play the cello had partly been dictated by the consideration that she would, with her parents and sister, complete the familial string quartet. I had taken a few not very successful dancing lessons since coming up and they were just about sufficient to enable me to invite Ruth to a May Ball in Trinity. These celebrations, which are a feature of

With Ruth at her sister's wedding

'May Week' (in fact in Cambridge tradition, a fortnight of summer roses and wine taking place in June, after Tripos exams are over), have become very elaborate over the years, but in our day the resources deployed were modest, no more than a dance band and a piper for some reels, plus a slap-up supper in the College Hall. The reels I enjoyed much more than the conventional ballroom dancing, where my shaky sense of rhythm tended to make me unrelaxed. Ruth took me in return to the Girton Ball. Marriage still lay some years ahead, but the idea began to form in the back of my mind well before it could seem to be a practical possibility.

4

Research Student

Ruth and I both graduated in June 1952. She then went off to do a post-graduate course in mathematical statistics at University College, London, subsequently being employed as a statistician in industry, while I remained in Cambridge to begin working for a PhD in theoretical physics. I had chosen the branch of that subject that is concerned with elementary particle physics, the study of the behaviour of the smallest constituents of matter. There was a small band of people in Cambridge working in that area, ranging in seniority from the impressive figure of Paul Dirac to four complete novices – Roger Phillips, Ron Shaw, John Taylor and me. The group met during term time at a weekly seminar that took place in a spare room in the Arts School, the building in which lectures were given for the Mathematical Tripos. The walls of the room were lined with a series of glass cases housing an extensive collection of mathematical models, plaster casts of interesting geometrical objects such as a variety of kinds of ruled surface, which had been assembled, I would guess, in the early years of the twentieth century, and which now had rather a faded and antiquarian air about them. There was also one of those blackboards that one can find all over the world, on which a visiting lecturer called Albert Einstein had written some speculative equations, which were then preserved for posterity by being sprayed with clear varnish.

At one end of the room were three comfortable chairs, invariably occupied by Dirac, Kemmer and a third university lecturer in our area, Jim Hamilton. The rest of us perched on rather uncomfortable chairs set out around the sides of the room, so that one had to keep one's head turned in order to be able to see the speaker. I have to say that the proceedings were not particularly well organized. The programme was more or less improvised, with the next topic quite often being chosen only a week or so ahead. Sometimes senior people would speak about their own work, and there was an occasional visiting speaker from outside, but the proceedings could also take the form of a research student reporting on some paper that he (and we were all male at that time) had recently been reading. Dirac would usually appear to go straight to sleep, but appearances could be deceptive and he would quite often open an eye at some stage of the proceedings and make a penetrating remark. These seminar meetings were certainly better than nothing, but I can see very clearly with hindsight that we tyros were not getting the best introduction to our chosen subject. Generally speaking, the Cambridge group was operating at some remove from the most exciting action.

For the rest of the time, we novice graduate students retreated to our College rooms, or to the library of the Cambridge Philosophical Society, which had an excellent collection of scientific periodicals, and we tried to do some research. Each of us had a supervisor with whom we would have occasional individual contact. Mine was Nick Kemmer. Before the war he had made some very important discoveries, the chief of which (an idea called 'isotopic spin') was proving to be the seed from which a good deal of further insight was to grow, though he did not contribute personally to these later developments. Kemmer originated from a Russian family that had lived for many years in Germany, and he only came to work in Britain in the mid-1930s. Perhaps as a consequence of this 'alien' provenance, Kemmer appeared not to have had a very good wartime experience, for he had not been given the opportunity to use his considerable talents in any very significant way. Nick was an exceptionally nice man, well liked by all who knew him, but by the time I became his research student he seemed to have lost his nerve about physics research. His understanding of fundamental principles was as deep as ever, but he did not do anything original with it, or even venture actively to help beginners in a modest way to find a problem that they might be able to tackle.

Much later, when I was the senior member of a large and active research group working in Cambridge on elementary particle physics, I used at the beginning of each academic year to give an avuncular talk to the latest crop of research students. The aim was to try to help them get used to the fact that their new life would inevitably have its ups and downs and it would be very different from the undergraduate study of an agreed syllabus. I could honestly say to them that my own first year as a research student had been the most miserable year of my life. It is often very hard to get going in research. In undergraduate work, a hard problem – even a Besicovitch problem – would probably yield after no more than a week's struggle, and at least you knew that the problem should have an accessible solution. In research the timescale is quite different; months of wrestling with difficulty may be necessary before any progress can be made, and you never know for sure whether you have chosen a sensible problem to tackle that can reasonably be expected to give useful results using the techniques you have at your disposal. These difficulties never wholly disappear from the life of theoretical research, but once you have gained a bit of experience, you acquire a degree of confidence that at least some of the time you will be able to get something done. At the beginning, particularly if you are not lucky enough to have a supervisor able to suggest a problem that might be manageable, life can be very bleak and frustrating. At the end of my first postgraduate year, essentially I had achieved nothing.

Fortunately, things began to brighten up in my second year. One of the big recent developments in our subject had been renormalization theory, a technique for getting sensible (and, it turned out, very accurate) results out of quantum field theory, the standard formalism to use in discussing the behaviour of small and fast-moving elementary particles. I noticed that there was still one small point that had not been covered in the initial pioneering work, but which seemed worth taking a look at. The big original discoveries had treated the processes concerned as if they were taking place over an infinite time-span. This was a sensible simplification to make, since the times involved were certainly very long compared with the relevant basic timescales for the interaction, but for completeness it seemed worth making sure that the move from infinity to the actually realistic case of a very long time interval would not upset the consistency of the rather delicate mathematical manipulations that were needed to obtain sensible results. This proved to be a fairly simple problem to sort out satisfactorily. I decided to use this work as the basis for a submission in the next Trinity Research Fellowship competition. Once a year the College offered about five four-year Fellowships, open to all its members of a standing of less than four years' postgraduate research, the awards to be made solely on the grounds of the quality of original work submitted. It was a bit of a risk putting in after only two years' research, since most candidates waited to take advantage of the full three years permitted, but I decided to have a go. I kept my candidature secret from my parents, as I did not want them to be disappointed if I were unsuccessful. I travelled back to Cambridge on the day in early October when the results were to be announced, and I arrived in College to find that I had been elected. Immediately I sent a telegram home telling Mother and Father the good news. My pleasure was great at this achievement, for a Prize Fellowship (as these awards were usually called in Trinity) had been the start of many successful academic careers. There were two other new Research Fellows from my own year, Michael Atiyah (later to win a Fields Medal, the nearest equivalent in maths to a Nobel Prize, for his work in topology) and John Elliott (a distinguished historian of Spain), and two more from the year ahead of us.

Earlier in my second year, another significant event had been a change of supervisor. Nick Kemmer had left Cambridge to take up a professorship in Edinburgh, and his successor was a Pakistani theorist, Abdus Salam. Abdus was quite a different person from Nick, much younger and bubbling over with new ideas, some very good (he later won a Nobel Prize), and some, frankly, not so good. Like many ebulliently fertile thinkers, Salam was not always able to tell the good from the bad. He once said to me, 'Publish all your ideas. People will remember the good ones and forget the bad.' Even as a young man, I could see that this was not good advice. About the same time, another Cambridge theorist, a bit older than me and with a distinguished career ahead of him, told me, 'Don't read other people's papers – it will only spoil your originality.' I knew that I was certainly not creative enough to do without the stimulus of the ideas of others.

Oddly enough, when Salam took me over, he did not suggest any particular problem for me to work on. Nevertheless, the air of activity that surrounded him, and his international involvement with other leading players in our field, created an atmosphere that was stimulating for us beginners. Our little group in Cambridge had been drawn nearer to the scene of the action. With inevitable stops and starts still to come, my research career had begun to develop.

Becoming a Fellow of Trinity not only translated me from the arid land of student food to the pleasant pastures of the High Table (I put on half a stone in my first term as a Fellow), but it provided a significantly enhanced income, guaranteed for four years. This enabled Ruth and me to contemplate realistically the possibility of marriage, the realization of the life-long commitment to each other that had been growing in our minds. We had, of course, kept in close touch after she had left Cambridge. It was still an age in which regular letter-writing was practised. (After marriage, when sometimes I was working away from home for a period, I would write something to Ruth every day, even if it took time to accumulate enough to fill a full letter – nothing is easier than such a chronicle, where anything that happens is grist to the epistolary mill and the letter is just like ordinary conversation.) We had days out together and visits to each other's families. It now seems a rather quaint thing to have to report, but I formally proposed to her, slipping an engagement ring on her finger, during a day out at the Quorn Hunt Point to Point, while she was staying with my family in Grantham.

We were married in Ruth's parish church of St James the Great, Friern Barnet, on 26 March 1955. It was the beginning of a union of mutual support, love and happiness together which, through the inevitable ups

Our wedding day

and downs of life, has been of absolutely central significance for me.

We spent our honeymoon on the Isles of Scilly. These beautiful small islands off the westernmost tip of Cornwall, kept unspoilt by the fortunate fact of a limited water supply that inhibits over-development, became a great favourite with us. We have had many wonderful holidays on Scilly, later with our children and later still with our grandchildren.

On our return from honeymoon, we lived for a few months in a College flat above a sports shop belonging to the family of the famous cricketer, Jack Hobbs. I took my PhD in the summer and soon thereafter we were packing up to leave Cambridge to cross the Atlantic for the first of many times, so that I could take up a postdoctoral fellowship at the California Institute of Technology in Pasadena.

5

Caltech

Ruth and I crossed the Atlantic by what was then the cheapest route, by liner from Liverpool to New York. We had to spend the night before embarkation in a Liverpool hotel and we took the opportunity this gave us to make a round trip on the overhead railway that then encircled the city docks. Scorning the expense, we bought first-class tickets, costing 1s 6d, rather than the second-class fare of 1s (about 7p rather than 5p in present money). The transatlantic voyage lasted about six days and it provided a relaxing interlude, with plenty of good food and an attendant to wrap you up in a blanket when you chose to recline in a deckchair. Clocks were only put back an hour a night, so there was no problem of jet-lag to contend with. Arrival in New York carried us up the Hudson, after passing the Statue of Liberty and the Battery, a perfect way to approach the city.

Ruth had an aunt and uncle who lived in New Jersey and so we stayed a week or two with them before setting out west. Switching on the television set one evening, I saw four young men in tuxedos appear on the screen, who began to sing in close harmony the ditty 'Give me that old time religion'. I began to realize that the Christian scene in the States was going to have a somewhat different tone from that which we were used to back home.

We travelled out to Pasadena by rail, crossing the continent on a super-train, the *California Zephyr*, equipped with observation domes and what seemed to us a very expensive dining car. The train's timetable was arranged so that on one day we crossed the Rockies in daylight, and the next day the Sierra Nevadas, while traversing the duller plains of the Midwest and the desert of Utah during the night. Arriving at Pasadena, we settled into an apartment that we had taken over from some English friends who had been at Caltech the year before. We also acquired their somewhat elderly car, a Kaiser made by a firm that had built Liberty ships during the war but which did not survive long in the postwar automobile business. We had very friendly and helpful neighbours, one of whom was our landlady, Miss Miller. She continued a custom that she had followed with our predecessors, of inviting us round once a week to watch *The $64,000 Question* on television. We enjoyed this apparently fraught competition, but we were shocked and disappointed to learn later that some of the most nail-biting moments had, in fact, been fixed beforehand.

I had not acquired a British driving licence at home, though I had had some lessons, and so an immediate task was to prepare to take the State of California test. First, you had to pass a written exam, most of whose multiple-choice questions were at the level of difficulty represented by 'When the traffic lights change, do you (a) blow your horn and hope for the best; (b) press down on the accelerator, shouting 'Get out of the way'; (c) come to a controlled halt?' Then followed the more exacting part, the actual driving test. I had been helped to prepare for this by our neighbour on the other side from Miss Miller, who most kindly spent time accompanying me on my practice drives, as the law required some qualified driver to do. When it came to the time of the test, you queued up until you were at the front and a tester had got in the car with you. The test then began as you drove over a yellow line just in front. Feeling a little flustered, I accidentally put the car into reverse rather than forward, and so gently bumped the car behind. My amiable tester told me to calm down and said that, since I had not crossed the yellow line, the test had not yet officially started. With such generous encouragement, I was able to pull myself together and duly passed.

Because initially we were not fluent in using our car, on our first

After the tension of the driving test, we grew fond of the car

Sunday Ruth and I went to a church a couple of blocks up the road, rather than attempting to seek out the Episcopalian congregation in Pasadena that would have been our natural ecclesiastical home. The church we had chosen turned out to be United Presbyterian. We received such a warm welcome, and found such a worshipful atmosphere, that we decided there and then to become honorary Presbyterians during our stay in Pasadena.

Living in the United States taught me something that I had not fully realized before: that I am a European. We received a great deal of kindness and help from the people we met in America, and over the years we were to come to have a number of close friends in the United States, but we also recognized that Americans are different. For many of them the focus of their attention and knowledge appeared to be astonishingly limited to the North American scene. The instant friendliness, so frequently displayed in casual encounters, sometimes seemed to be accompanied by a degree of superficiality and a certain lack of subtlety in judgement. America often appeared to be a land of sharply contrasted opinions, rather than the 'shades of grey' of the European spectrum, with its many possible intermediate positions. From time to time I found myself getting together with some French postdocs at Caltech to chew over the oddnesses of the Americans. Of course, I know that there were some tricks of perspective involved here, together with some repressed homesickness, and that, had we been in Britain, no doubt those Frenchmen would have been chatting surreptitiously with American colleagues about the peculiarities of the Brits.

Caltech was only a short distance away from our apartment. I had gone there to work with Murray Gell-Mann, one of the world's outstanding theoretical physicists. Although Murray was only a few years older than me, he already had a glittering international reputation and he would eventually go on to win a Nobel Prize for his work on the quark structure of matter. My nine months spent in interacting with him were a transformative experience for me, through which I began to grasp something more about the nature of research in theoretical physics. In addition to his intellectual brilliance, two aspects of Murray's character stood out. One was that he was a polymath who really liked you to know that, and who could talk authoritatively about pretty well any subject except sport. One of his particular interests was ornithology. Many years later Murray and his wife visited us in the President's Lodge in Queens' College. I showed them around some of the rooms of that splendid fifteenth-/sixteenth-century building, while Murray instructed me on the history of the College. For him, however, what seemed to be the high point of the visit came when he spotted an Edwardian collection of stuffed birds, mounted in a glass dome. His eyes lit up as he rushed over to identify all those highly coloured specimens from South America.

A second Gell-Mann characteristic was one that contrasted strongly with my experiences with Salam. Murray not only had very good ideas, but he did all that he could to ensure that any idea expressed in public was one that was going to stand up to criticism and endure. Not for him a scatter-gun approach in which only some shots would hit the target. The Gell-Mann weapon was the rifle, trained on the bullseye.

At the time that I came within Murray's orbit, a debate was beginning in particle physics about what would be the best way in which to formulate theory. The traditional resource had been quantum field theory, and through the success of the renormalization programme this had yielded wonderfully accurate results in the case of quantum electrodynamics (QED), the theory describing interactions between photons (particles of light) and electrons. But now experimental interest was shifting to a different kind of interaction, the so-called strong force that controlled the behaviour of protons and neutrons, the constituents of nuclear matter. This force was mediated by particles called mesons, in some respects the counterparts of photons, but techniques analogous to those used in QED did not work at all well in strong force calculations. Consequently quite a few theorists had become disillusioned with quantum field theory. Perhaps it tried to do too much. A field is spread out over the whole of space and it varies in time. However, experimental access is much more limited than that: actual empirical information is derived from scattering experiments, in which you know what goes in and you measure what comes out, but you do not have any accurate knowledge of what has been going on in between. During the war, Werner Heisenberg had suggested that a leaner formalism than quantum field theory might be more appropriate, expressed in terms of what he called the S[cattering]-matrix. This idea had recently been revived and the S-matrix approach was being vigorously pushed, particularly by a charismatic theorist, Geoffrey Chew, working at the University of California at Berkeley. Gell-Mann was interested in this project but, characteristically, he did not commit himself to it with the unbridled enthusiasm displayed by Chew. Nevertheless Murray wished to maintain some sort of connection with developments in S-matrix theory. The approach was based on exploiting certain mathematical properties (technically, the analytic structure of scattering amplitudes) that were known to hold for the case of scattering with two particles in/two particles out. Murray suggested to me that I should see if I could find an appropriate generalization of these properties to the multiparticle case, which would correspond to the production of extra particles in the course of the scattering process. This I was able to do (though, with hindsight, I can see that I did not find the most transparent way of expressing the result). This work was the major fruit of my time at Caltech, coupled with my learning a lot more in a general way about particle physics. This increase in professional knowledge came principally from lectures and seminars given not only by Gell-Mann, but also by an older colleague of his at Caltech, Richard Feynman. Feynman was also someone who would prove to be a future Nobel Prize winner, and he has become well known to a wider public through his popular writings, which combine deep physical insight with a rather relentlessly jokey style.

You could hardly find two people more different in temperament and manner than Feynman and Gell-Mann. Each cultivated a public persona. For Murray it was the cultured polymath; for Dick it was the fun-loving, bongo drum-playing person who just happened to be a brilliant physicist. It could be funny to listen to them talking together, as they played off each other. Gell-Mann, of course, always pronounced foreign names in the correct indigenous fashion and this would provoke Feynman to pretend that he did not understand what had been said. Both were very great physicists, but even here there was a difference of style. Feynman was a great calculator – he discovered a technique, universally called Feynman integrals, which is perhaps the most powerful weapon in the armoury of the modern theorist – while Gell-Mann was more a conceptual innovator, whose greatest discovery was the formulation of the quark theory of matter, describing the properties of the constituents out of which particles such as protons and neutrons have turned out to be made. Each respected the other, but I think that there was also an element of rivalry, and of suppressed envy of the other's different talent and achievements, present in their relationship.

During my time at Caltech, I discovered how one can derive intellectual benefit from working with a genius of strong character. You had to interact with him, but also you had to keep your distance. Spending too long in Murray's presence would simply prove too overwhelming. He would impose his view on you totally and, of course, he could always out-think you. What one had to do was to get a general idea of where he thought the next point of significant advance might lie, and then retreat for a while to see if one could identify some modest aspect that might lie within one's limited competence to investigate, and then get on with it on one's own, before presenting this offering to its inspirer.

After I had been at Caltech a few months, I attended a meeting of the American Physical Society, held in Los Angeles, at which the discovery of the antiproton was announced. In the early 1930s Dirac had predicted the existence of antimatter, and in the case of the electron this was almost immediately confirmed by the discovery of its antiparticle, the positron. Because protons are much more massive than electrons, it was much more difficult to produce antiprotons, and this only became an experimental feasibility in the mid-1950s with the construction of a large accelerator, the Bevatron, at Berkeley. Duly the expected discovery was made, and the two leading physicists involved soon received shares in a Nobel Prize. Looking back on it, this was perhaps not as exciting an event as it appeared at the time. What would have been truly significant would have been if there had been no antiproton, for that would have caused a deep crisis in theoretical physics. Many of the most important advances in physics have arisen from having to come to terms with the wholly unexpected.

While I was getting deeper into particle physics, Ruth was also working at Caltech as an assistant operating a mass spectrometer used in the geology department for carbon-dating. Come the beginning of June 1956, however, we were packing up to leave Pasadena. I had come to the USA on a Commonwealth Fund Fellowship (now rightly called a Harkness Fellowship to acknowledge the generosity of the donor who had endowed the Foundation). It incorporated a hands-across-the-sea element in it, so that it was part of the Fellowship's purpose that holders should really get to know the United States before returning home. You were therefore *required* to spend three months travelling. This was a wonderful condition to which to be subjected. I am very much a Protestant work-ethic type of person, for whom the idea of a three-month holiday would have been inconceivable had it not been compulsory. We travelled extensively in our rattling old Kaiser (a perpetual source of anxiety to me, but as it turned out, in fact a staunch performer), particularly enjoying the great National Parks, such as Yosemite, Yellowstone and the Grand Tetons, as well as visiting many of the great cities of the Midwest and the East. It was a marvellous experience. As this fruitful and

With Nick Kemmer at a Rochester Conference. I had recently written some critical reviews of recent publications. On meeting me, the Russian in the picture commented: 'You look kinder than your book reviews!'

varied North American year approached its end, it became apparent what lay next ahead for us. In the course of our travels I had received a cable offering me a lectureship in Nick Kemmer's Institute of Theoretical Physics in Edinburgh. This would be a permanent job, my first secure rung on the academic ladder, and I promptly cabled back my grateful acceptance.

6

University Teacher

———————

When we arrived in Edinburgh and I took up my University lectureship, a new phase began in my life. While acquisition of knowledge is truly a life-long pursuit, for the academic there is a particular period of apprenticeship and intellectual formation that is the indispensable preliminary to the commencement of a full professional career. That preparatory phase ended for me when I left Caltech. I now had to practise the art of combining continued research with the daily tasks of a university teacher. I soon came to value this mixed intellectual economy, since, like many other people, I found that I did not get enough good original ideas to sustain me in a life of undiluted research. I have known a number of people who have been permanent professors at the Institute for Advanced Study at Princeton. These prestigious appointments impose upon their holders no set duties, for the professors are simply free to pursue their own thoughts in whatever direction they may wish. In particular, the Institute is a student-free zone. For some this proved to be the perfect life and they used the opportunities thus provided to very fruitful effect. However, for others – and this could include people of Nobel calibre – it seemed as if the burden of unremittingly having to be thinking great thoughts all the time eventually proved less than ideal, and after some years they returned to normal university life. If the need for a teaching dimension of some kind was true for academics of that distinction, how much more would it be likely to be true for the rest of us. Very often weeks can go by in research work without any obvious progress resulting, but if one has also done some teaching during that time, one at least feels some satisfaction at the thought that something worthwhile has been achieved.

I suppose that I was particularly conscious of the value of a teaching dimension to life because by temperament I am a very pedagogic kind of person. I simply like telling people things and thereby handing on the torch of knowledge. If someone approaches me in the street and asks the way to somewhere, and I know it and am able to give them directions, I quit the encounter with a warm inner glow, feeling that something of good has been accomplished.

Consequently I took to lecturing like a duck to water and, to be perfectly honest, I felt that I was reasonably effective at it. I believe myself to be a lively speaker, perhaps more intent on stimulating the interest of my hearers than worried about meticulously laying out the smallest details of the argument, relentlessly stacked up in sober, logical sequence. It is the shape of ideas that intrigues me. I sought to persuade my classes to listen to me, rather than scribbling it down all the time in the hope of thinking about the sense later. When the handing out of duplicated lecture notes eventually became a persistent student demand to university teachers, I responded simply by giving them detailed page references to material already in standard textbooks that would treat the matter in the same way that I was following in the lectures. I feel very strongly that one of the skills one has to cultivate at university is that of gaining knowledge by reading for oneself. Of course, I recognized that I had to write on the board the main equations of the argument, and that the students would need to copy these down, but I wanted the process of transcription from my writing in chalk to their writing in a notebook to proceed via the mind and not merely by hand and ear.

Perhaps it sounds as though my technique may have been a bit broad brush and informal, and maybe up to a point it was. I suspect that I was more effective with the better students, though when I returned to Cambridge and taught pairs of undergraduates in supervisions, I always tried to make a special effort to help those who were finding things difficult,

Musing at an Alpine summer school

and there was very great satisfaction when, after some effort on both sides, you saw a little light go on in someone's mind. Anyway it is certainly a gift to me when today, as sometimes happens, a person comes up to me after a public lecture and says, with some appearance of pleasant remembrance, 'I went to your lectures on quantum mechanics in 19XX.' Lecturers in mathematical subjects vary across a stylistic spectrum from those who simply copy out equations from notes onto the blackboard (usually at the same time talking with their back to the class), to those who try for a bit more by way of rhetorically conveyed influence. I aspired to be at the more performance-oriented end of the business.

One of the results of the contemporary teaching assessment exercises now imposed on universities is that they tend to urge lecturers to adopt particular techniques and the technology that goes with them (handouts, overheads, PowerPoint), with the aim of producing a standard style, in a way that is, in fact, discouraging to an educationally effective range of stimulating idiosyncrasy. The teachers who really influenced me were certainly a varied bunch, not conforming to a single stereotype. I remember Murray Gell-Mann once talking to me about his experience of lecturers when he was in graduate school. One of them (Julian Schwinger) delivered masterfully ordered orations, whose Macaulay-esque prose never contained a subordinate clause that did not duly close.

One might be enthralled at the time, but afterwards the effects of such perfection seemed to fade away rather quickly. Another lecturer (Vicky Weisskopf) would come in, write an equation on the board, scratch his head and say, 'That can't be right', correct it, and gradually, if apparently erratically, build up an argument whose structure then stayed in the mind of the listener long after the lecture was over, precisely because it had not been presented as a smoothed-out *fait accompli*.

There was a second dimension to university teaching in addition to my undergraduate lecturing that I enjoyed a lot: the supervision of research students working for a PhD. I believe it is fair to say that by the time I was given this responsibility, the quality of life for the graduate student was considerably better than that which had been experienced by myself and my contemporaries. I wanted to be of real assistance to the beginners in my charge, and so I tried to suggest a problem for a starting student to tackle that would be worthwhile, but also likely to be do-able using the techniques being developed in our research group. Even the best people, it seemed to me, needed some apprentice period before they were ready to move over to being fully self-propelled. The most difficult students I had were one or two of quite obvious intrinsic ability who declined a humble start to their research and wanted instead to get down to struggling with the big problems straight away. Such attempted precocity proved unlikely to be a recipe for the success that was hoped for.

Another respect in which the lot of the graduate student had improved over that of my own student days in Cambridge, was that it was lived out in a real community and not in the isolation of college rooms. Both at Edinburgh and a little later at Cambridge, there were now research groups whose members worked in the same building and whose collective activities included a properly organized seminar pro-gramme with the regular participation of external speakers, together with daily opportunities for continual interplay through mingling at group sessions of morning coffee and afternoon tea. Of course there were still frustrations and difficulties for those attempting research for the first time, and a supervisor needed a degree of pastoral awareness and a willingness to offer a friendly listening ear to those who were struggling. I remember having several chats with a young man who was a member of our group, but not one of my own students. He had experienced unusual difficulty in getting started and was understandably discouraged. Several of us sought to persuade him to stick it out a bit longer. He did so, and he is now a Fellow of the Royal Society.

In my 23 years as a university teacher of theoretical physics, I supervised 27 PhD students, as well as a few others that I took over for short periods while their regular supervisor was absent. I enjoyed these close relationships very much. Three of my former students have become Fellows of the Royal Society and all of them got their degrees, though one or two did so without too much to spare. I am grateful to all these erstwhile students for their friendship, and I look back on our times together as having been among the most satisfying aspects of my academic career.

I had only spent two years in Edinburgh before being invited in 1958 to return to Cambridge as a University Lecturer. Promotion to Reader followed in 1965, and in 1968 I was elected the first holder of a newly established Professorship of Mathematical Physics. At the time of my return, Trinity had appointed me a College Teaching Fellow and so, in addition to my university duties, I did the standard load of six hours a week supervision of undergraduates reading for the Maths Tripos. This intimate and personal form of teaching certainly had its satisfactions, but over the years it increasingly came also to have its *longueurs*. The problem was its repetitiveness. If, say, you were supervising quantum mechanics that term, a good deal of the time you spent with your 12 supervisees would be taken up with going over the same material six times. There is not the variety of point of view and difference of response in the case of theoretical physics that one might find in pupils studying history or theology. I have to admit to a significant degree of relief when my becoming a professor disqualified me from further supervising and I was given the almost free-ride in College that is allowed to Professorial Fellows.

The most precociously brilliant undergraduate that I ever taught was Brian Josephson, whom I supervised for a term in quantum mechanics.

(I can also claim to have taught the same subject to Martin Rees, later Master of Trinity and President of the Royal Society.) Josephson had got a Scholarship to Trinity at an incredibly early age and when he came up he was still unusually young. Perhaps because of this, he was a very quiet student. He never had any difficulty with any of the problems I set him and so I had to struggle to find other ways of filling up our time together. This did not turn out to be easy. The conversation did not flow, and when I came to write my end-of-term report on him, I did not feel at all sure what to say. I settled for something to the effect that he was an absolute wizard at technique, but I was uncertain about initiative and originality. Within a few years, Josephson had become a Nobel laureate! I find it a useful spiritual exercise occasionally to recall this spectacular error of judgement.

I had another, but less embarrassing, connection with Josephson when he was a candidate for a Trinity Research Fellowship. The College's custom was that each candidate had a 'manager', who was the Fellow charged with presenting that particular person's case to the other electors. The manager was chosen to be as near as possible in expertise to the candidate's field, but obviously it was not always possible to get a really close match. I was Brian's manager, despite the fact that his area of theoretical physics (condensed matter) was very different from my own. I had got expert referees' reports on his dissertation that were superlative in tone, but before the final meeting of the electors I noticed a paper in *Physical Review Letters* by John Bardeen, the grand old man of condensed matter physics and the only person to have won two Nobel Prizes in physics, which said that Josephson was wrong. It was far beyond my powers to adjudicate the matter, but I assured the electors that if Josephson had made a mistake, I felt sure that it was a much more creative act than the correct work of most other people. Fortunately they accepted this and Brian was elected. A few weeks later, Bardeen withdrew his objections, and this was the work for which Josephson not too long afterwards was awarded his Nobel Prize.

Shortly after I had returned to Cambridge, the Faculty of Mathematics was transformed from a loose collection of College-based dons into something more coherent, by being divided in 1959 into two Departments, pure and applied, and each gradually acquired a consolidated set of buildings. I was a founder member of the Department of Applied Mathematics and Theoretical Physics, acronymically reduced to DAMTP and rendered pronounceable by transposing the last two letters to form 'Dampt'. The founding Head of our Department was George Batchelor, an expatriate Australian whose academic speciality was fluid mechanics, a subject that located him on the Applied Maths, or classical physics, side of the Department, while I was on the Theoretical Physics, or quantum, side of things.

George and I became good friends and for many years we played squash together every Friday evening. Neither of us was any good, but squash is a game in which you can have a lot of fun provided your partner is as bad as you are. After two or three games we would sit on the floor of the court for a rest and a brief chat about departmental affairs before resuming our exertions. George was a distinguished individual researcher, particularly in the difficult field of turbulent fluid motion, but he also came to have other important academic achievements to his credit. One was that he had played the leading role in bringing DAMTP into being and forming its initial departmental culture; another was founding and editing *The Journal of Fluid Mechanics*, which rapidly established itself as a premier periodical with a high standing in its area (and with a reputation for unhesitatingly requiring authors to revise their papers if the presentation was deemed unclear or otherwise unsatisfactory); the third was a highly successful and influential textbook, long in gestation, devoted to fluid mechanics. However, the same dedicated care and commitment that enabled George to play his widely creative roles so effectively also meant that he found it very difficult to let go of any of them. In the Department this led to problems with some colleagues.

The academic range of DAMTP was very wide, for it contained a number of different active and internally cohesive research groups, operating under the one departmental umbrella. There was always going to be some tension between these groups about the sharing of resources, and in particular concerning which academic area was to be allocated any new post that might become available. I felt that on the whole our particle physics group was being treated fairly. George certainly knew his own mind and pressed the case for his point of view. That view might not always coincide with one's own, but I believed that we got a fair hearing and a reasonable share of what was going. A somewhat older colleague in our group, Richard Eden, was less persuaded that this was so, and Fred Hoyle, the Plumian Professor of Astronomy and the leading figure of a large astrophysics and cosmology group, was decidedly less content. Fred was a brilliant scientist – he certainly should have been given a share in a Nobel Prize for his work on stellar nucleogenesis, the processes in the stars by which the chemical elements are made – but he could also sometimes be a bit of a maverick, both scientifically and in relations with his colleagues. There was a stubborn streak in Fred, and once he had taken a stance he would persist in it whatever arguments to the contrary might be produced.

The Head of our Department was appointed every five years by the Faculty Board of Mathematics. In 1964, George Batchelor came up for possible reselection, but Fred and Richard felt that already it was time for a change. I was on the Faculty Board at that time and took the opposite view, believing that George deserved at least a second term, which he himself certainly desired. I considered Batchelor to be the best available candidate, and I believed that he should be given the opportunity to consolidate the work he had done in getting the Department formed. In the upshot, George was reappointed by a convincing majority, but Fred soon left DAMTP to sulk in his tent at a new (and as it turned out, highly successful) Institute of Theoretical Astronomy that had been set up, essentially to keep him in Cambridge, while Richard transferred to the Department of Physics (Cavendish Laboratory). Along with many other colleagues in DAMTP, I regretted these departures but I felt that, given the personalities and circumstances, they had been more or less inevitable.

One of the good features of academic life in Cambridge was the institution of sabbatical leave. This was interpreted in accordance with

Enjoying a trip on Lake Geneva with John C. Taylor

biblical principles, allowing one term's leave in seven. Of course this time was not simply holiday, but rather it allowed one to concentrate on completing research projects and to spend time in other institutions in order to benefit from the different perspectives that they offered on one's subject. I gained a lot from regular visits to North American institutions (particularly Princeton, Berkeley and Stanford) and from spending time at the European Organization for Nuclear Research (CERN), the large laboratory for high energy physics, located just outside Geneva. Eventually I came to do a spell as one of the United Kingdom representatives on the CERN Council. The first thing one did at Council meetings was to fill in an expenses form. A lady then came round with a kind of supermarket trolley containing all the different currencies of the Member States and you were reimbursed on the spot in the currency of your choice. (Practically everyone asked for Swiss francs.) The only other place I have encountered this efficient system of instant repayment was at Committee meetings at the Royal Society.

CERN has been an outstandingly successful example of how to organize international collaboration in those expensive forms of science, such as experimental particle physics, which no European nation could afford to pursue on its own. It has been able to strike an acceptable balance between giving priority to projects of high significance irrespective of who had proposed them, while also allowing physicists from all the different Member States a reasonable degree of access to the joint facilities. At the time of writing CERN is about to bring on stream the LHC (Large Hadron Collider) which will be the highest energy experimental facility in the world. A tiny fraction of its budget is also sufficient to maintain a good quality Theory Division operating alongside the experimentalists.

7

Family

—=➤•◦•◄=—

Soon after we arrived in Edinburgh, Ruth and I bought a small house on a new housing estate at Fairmilehead, looking out towards the Pentland Hills. In 1957, our first child, Peter, was born in a city hospital with the rather grand-sounding name of The Simpson Memorial Maternity Pavilion. I remember very vividly when Peter and his mother came home for the first time – how small he looked and how uncertain we sometimes felt as parents of this tiny being who could not tell us in any articulate way what his needs were or how he was feeling. Of course we managed, as novice parents have to do, receiving some occasional help from a friendly neighbour who was a midwife and a source of useful advice. Gradually, we came to realize that young babies are more resilient than one might at first fear.

When we left Edinburgh to return to Cambridge, we decided that we must buy the largest house that we could afford, since we hoped our family would grow. Some new houses were being built by a very well-respected local builder on a plot of land to the south of the city, which before the war had been the University polo ground. It proved possible to buy one of these homes with the aid of a mortgage and a loan from the University, the price being £5,000 in 1959 money. This purchase was one of the best moves in our family life. Rutherford Road (that part of Cambridge belonged to Trinity and all its roads were named after distinguished members of the College) was a cul-de-sac, and most of the new houses were occupied by couples of our age who also had young families. As the children grew into toddlers and then schoolchildren, an active social life developed in our dead-end road, whose safety allowed for easy communal play.

Two more children were born in Cambridge, our daughter Isobel in 1959 and our younger son Michael in 1963. All our children are now themselves married and the next generation consists of nine much-loved grandchildren. A great deal of happiness came to Ruth and me from our family life, and we were given the additional blessing of three children-in-law, Jill, Timothy and Karen, whom we greatly liked and with whom we have always been on very good terms. As far as circumstances permitted (Michael and Karen lived in Australia for a number of years), we have endeavoured each year to have a week's family holiday together, as it is surely good for children to grow up knowing their cousins.

When Father retired, my parents had returned to Somerset to live in the small cathedral city of Wells. As a family, we visited them regularly, in particular usually being there at about Eastertide. Mother and Father were very fond of Ruth and of their grandchildren, so these were happy gatherings. I do not doubt that Mother always had in mind the need to avoid any whiff of the interfering attitude that had troubled relationships with her own mother-in-law. I believe that Ruth came to occupy in her affections something of the place which would have been that of my sister Ann had she lived, and she was certainly very pleased that Ruth, who had lost her own mother before we married, was willing from the start to call her 'Mother'.

Our life in Cambridge in the 1960s and 1970s followed a pattern that was common for the families of dons at that time. Ruth did not have a job, but she devoted herself to the home and the family full-time. Two evenings a week I did my college supervision teaching, staying on to dine in Hall afterwards. While the children were still young, they would be in bed already by the time I got home on those supervising days. At the time all this seemed just the natural rhythm of life, but looking back on it now I can see that it made life pretty easy for the husband and that the present-day style of a greater sharing of parental and domestic tasks has

Mother and Father with the children

much to be said for it. When I see my sons or my son-in-law setting to work on some domestic task, such as ironing, I not only admire their willingness, but I also feel a little guilty that such an action would have been unlikely to have occurred to me when I was their age. One thing I can claim, however, is that I did try to draw a clear line between work and home. I almost never brought work back to Rutherford Road, as I felt it was important that when I was there I was readily available to the family.

On those evenings when I was home early, I liked to take my turn at reading to the children before they went to bed. There is great pleasure to be had both in reading aloud and in being read to. We continued this family tradition well beyond the era of bedtime stories, by having sessions when we were on holiday. For a number of years we had some very good family holidays semi-camping with the aid of our Dormobile motor caravan, and it became a habit at tea-time in the van for me to read from a book by P. G. Wodehouse. I have happy memories of all of us being doubled up with laughter at some scrape in which Bertie Wooster had got caught up, all narrated in Wodehouse's wonderfully sprightly prose.

Bedtime readings had always ended with a Bible story, drawn from one of the many excellent collections that were available for children. As a family, we worshipped at Holy Trinity, one of the city-centre churches in Cambridge, chosen because it had splendid children's work, organized by two gifted and dedicated young women, Rosemary Farren and Marguerite Roberts. Ruth and I were anxious to help our children grow up in the faith (as, in fact, they did), but we were also anxious to give this help in the right way and to refrain from trying to shove Christianity down their throats whether they liked it or not. We devised a scheme which we believed combined the experience of regular worship with some exercise of individual choice. It was based on a two-week cycle. On the first Sunday we all went together to Holy Trinity, and attendance was compulsory unless you were unwell. On the second Sunday I went to the early Communion service in Trinity Chapel and Ruth went to the mid-morning service at Holy Trinity. The children could choose either to accompany her or to stay at home with their father, by then returned from College. There was a period, as I recall it, when Isobel always went on the optional Sundays and the two boys nearly always stayed at home. This system came to an end when I was away for a time working in America. Ruth explained to the children that worshipping in church every Sunday was essential for her, and this would only be possible while I was away if they always accompanied her. This they agreed to do. When I got back again, this wholly regular pattern had got established and accepted, and we did not revert to the old stop/start optional mode.

Every Sunday evening in term time, I went to Evensong in Trinity Chapel, again staying on to dine in Hall afterwards. In this way I heard Harry Williams preach all the sermons that compose *The True Wilderness*, in my opinion his greatest book. Even at the time, it was a powerful experience for me to listen to Harry, and I came, on later re-reading, to be able to 'hear' more of what he had to say.

Our children: Isobel, Michael and Peter

One Sunday evening, when I was just about to drive off to College, Ruth rushed to the window and indicated that she had something to tell me. She had just heard on the television news the announcement that Rab Butler was to be the next Master of Trinity. That evening in Hall was the quietest I ever experienced. We all sat there, largely silent, digesting the news that our next Master was not to be a Trinity man (the first outsider since Richard Bentley in the early eighteenth century), and that he was to be a retired politician rather than the customary distinguished academic. It all seemed a bit odd, possibly even a bit ominous. As it turned out, Rab proved an excellent Master for the later 1960s, since his political skills enabled him to steer the College away from the sort of troublesome confrontations with students that were a feature of that period in a number of other institutions.

Our children were all educated in the private system, starting at Byron House, with the boys going on to St Faith's and the Leys School, while Isobel went to the Perse School for Girls. I think one has to do the best one can as a parent to foster the particular abilities and interests of one's children. Our offspring were all academically bright and we judged it a good use of the money we had available to use it for them in this way. An additional reason for starting on the private route was that our elder son Peter has a congenital high-frequency hearing loss (long suspected by his parents, but only tardily diagnosed by the medical profession), and it was an obvious benefit for him to be in small classes.

Eventually the two boys went on to Cambridge, both choosing Trinity, a College big enough for one to be able to escape from the presence of a donnish father if necessary, and both studied for the Natural Sciences Tripos, though Peter switched to computer science for his final year. Isobel was the one who got away, going to The Queen's College, Oxford, to read history as a member of that College's first female intake in 1979. There she met an undergraduate reading mathematics, who was two years ahead of her in the College, Timothy Morland. They were married as soon as Isobel graduated, thereby becoming the first-ever wedded couple both of whom were members of Queen's.

Peter now looks after information technology for a City law firm. Isobel teaches children with special needs. Michael is an accountant working on the finance side of a middle-sized firm. It is a significant step, now well in our past, when one's family all become financially self-supporting. It is a matter for much greater satisfaction and gratefulness, when this independence is achieved without severing the bonds of family affection. In addition to our yearly week's holiday together, we also try to have a family visit to the theatre round about Christmas time. For many years this took the form of a trip to the satisfyingly traditional pantomime at the Theatre Royal, Wimbledon, but latterly, the increasing age and sophistication of the grandchildren has encouraged more adventurous possibilities. Reading books and seeing plays has always been an important part of our family life.

Literature and the theatre were not our only artistic interests. Ruth had grown up in a musical family and she played the cello in a number of local amateur orchestras, starting with CUMS (the Cambridge University Musical Society) when she was a student. Latterly she played

Ruth, in a pose uncannily like mine on page 25

a cello that she made for herself at a remarkable Cambridge workshop that teaches people how to make their own stringed instruments. My role has been as willing audience fodder. Michael is the only one of our children who took to musical pursuits with some seriousness, moving on from the clarinet to a variety of other wind instruments. We enjoyed buying pictures from time to time from local artists, until we ran out of wall space, also in demand in our home to accommodate book-shelves. One day I saw in a Sunday colour supplement some photo-graphs of ceramics made for the Carmelite Priory at Aylesford in Kent by a Polish émigré artist, Adam Kossowski. They were striking pieces of Christian art and I wrote to him to ask if he ever did work on a domestic scale. Mr Kossowski wrote back to invite me to visit him at his studio in London. I was most courteously received, being given a glass of sherry and feeling as though I were a minor Florentine merchant calling on a quattrocento Master. After some general conversation about the role of art in religion, he said to me, 'You are an Anglican, I suppose.' (He, of course, like most Poles, was a Roman Catholic.)

I acknowledged my ecclesiastical allegiance. He then said, 'Are you a believer?' I said that indeed I was, and after that we got on very well with each other. He agreed to make me a ceramic of the risen Christ, a powerful image which we were very glad to have in our home.

8

Scientific Career

—————➤◦◄—————

I greatly enjoyed my time working in theoretical elementary particle physics. I was fortunate in being in the subject during a period of particularly interesting development. It was an exciting time, even for a minor player in the game, with many unexpected puzzles and some mistakes on the way to eventual understanding. When I had started out as a research student in 1952, we believed nuclear matter to be made out of its obvious constituents, protons and neutrons. By the time I left particle physics in 1979, it had become clear that the protons and neutrons were themselves composites, made up of yet smaller and more fundamental entities. These were the celebrated quarks and gluons. Both these names illustrate the jokiness that came to characterize the terminology of particle physics, presumably as a minor source of relief from what otherwise might have seemed to be the subject's austerely abstracted nature.

Quarks are associated together in threes, and that relentlessly learned man Murray Gell-Mann, who was the dominant figure in the development of the quark idea, recalled a line from James Joyce's *Finnegan's Wake*, 'Three quarks for Muster Mark', which he then made use of in choosing the new nomenclature. Murray also tells us that he felt that there was a quart-pot atmosphere about the scene where the line occurs, and so he committed himself to a long-a pronunciation (to rhyme with corks), rather than the short-a pronunciation (to rhyme with sparks) that the euphony of the line seems to me clearly to demand. There is a still-persisting division in the world of elementary particle physicists about this issue – I continue to be a short-a man myself.

The joke associated with gluons is altogether more simple and straightforward, for it is the exchange of these particles that generates the force that makes the quarks stick together. In fact, so effective is this force that quarks are inextricably bound to each other and no one has ever succeeded in expelling a single isolated quark from within the particles that they constitute. A word is always a reassuring way to familiarize a strange fact, and so this state of unbreakably intense quark-togetherness is called the property of confinement.

You will see from this that physicists are quite prepared to trust in unseen realities, provided that the indirect motivations for the relevant belief are persuasive. In the quark case, these reasons for belief were twofold. One was that the patterns of the intrinsic properties displayed by particles that are directly observable, such as protons and neutrons, together with a whole slew of short-lived particles identified as products in high-energy interactions, corresponded in a beautiful way to just those that are possessed by the structures that can be built out of sets of quarks. (This insight was one of Gell-Mann's greatest achievements, including the successful prediction of the existence of hitherto un-observed particles needed to complete the patterns.) The second line of evidence related to experiments in which very high energy projectiles collided with target particles and were found to be deflected through large angles, a process that is called deep inelastic scattering. The extreme circumstances of the experiments (large energy, large momen-tum transfer) produced simplicity in the analysis. The observed behav-iour turned out to be readily interpretable as due to the projectiles having bounced off small 'hard' constituents sitting inside the target. When the details of deep inelastic scattering processes were looked at, it was found that they corresponded exactly to these internal scattering centres being quarklike in their character. This kind of argument had a venerable history, for Ernest Rutherford had used a similar kind of analysis in 1911, applied on a different scale, as the basis for his great discovery of the point-like positively charged nucleus lying at the centre of the atom.

It would not be appropriate here to try to describe in any detail the history of particle physics as it developed over the years, leading by the mid-1970s to what is now called the 'Standard Model' of quark structure. The focus of this book is more narrowly personal. I shall try shortly to indicate in a generally accessible way the kinds of problems that I worked on in my research career, but before doing so I want to say something about a different kind of scientific project, oriented towards the general educated reader. I believe that science is too interesting and significant a subject to be the closed preserve of the experts alone. Fundamental physics is an important part of human cultural achievement in which all should be able to share to the extent that it may prove possible for them to do so. This opening up of a significant intellectual heritage also requires that attempts at interdisciplinary sharing have to extend beyond the particularities of any specific branch of science, such as particle physics, to include also the underlying concepts that control the nature of the discourse, such as the ideas of quantum mechanics. Consequently I have also written two books for the layperson about the general ideas of quantum theory, as well as two books about particle physics.

The first of my quantum books was *The Quantum World* (1984). It has proved to be the best-selling of all my writings, its total sales getting into six figures, including a Japanese translation that has turned out to do remarkably well. When I received a copy of this translation, of course I could not check its contents but I opened the pages to take a look. Initially I was dismayed by what I saw, since I had not realized that books in Japanese, like books in Hebrew, are to be read from the back forward. Once this had been sorted out, another surprise awaited me. My Japanese publishers had garnished the edition with illustrations that had not been there in the English version. These portrayed the great founding figures of the subject, such as Heisenberg and Dirac, in terms of what I take to be a distinctively Japanese iconography. The subjects either leaned sharply forward or sharply back, and from their heads there emerged rays of light, no doubt denoting their elevated intellectual status.

My second quantum book appeared in 2002 in an Oxford University Press series called 'Very Short Introductions', in which an author has 30,000 words to cover a pretty large topic. I found this an interesting challenge, and I decided that my VSI *Quantum Theory* should have no equations in its main text, though I did put a few in a short mathematical Appendix for the hardier reader.

I have enjoyed having a go at projects involving semi-popular science writing, for which I think there are two important rules. One is to think very carefully about what you can explain and what the reader will have to take on trust. What is to be left out of the detailed treatment is as important a decision as what is to be put in. The other rule is to be scrupulous in making as clear as possible where one is reporting mainstream understandings with which all in the field would be happy to agree, and where one is reporting interesting but speculative and uncertain ideas. I know from my own reading, say in biology, how impossible it is for inexpert readers to make that judgement for themselves. I believe that there is too much 'gee-whizz' science writing that does not respect the obligation to come clean about the status of what is being talked about.

My first book about particle physics itself was called *The Particle Play* (1979) and it was completed during my last two years as a Cambridge professor. It presents the ideas of the Standard Model, using a sustained theatrical metaphor. Without becoming a best-seller, it was reasonably successful with the public for whom it was intended. *Particle Play* gives an account of where we had found ourselves when the dust had finally settled on that phase of particle physics during which I had been an active participant. A little later, I felt that it would be worthwhile to give a stage-by-stage account of how we had got there. In other words, I wanted to guide the reader through the dust storms that had preceded the final clearing of the view. I also felt that it would be useful to give an account of those stirring times from the perspective – if I may now adopt a military metaphor – of the ordinary foot-soldier, rather than the public having to rely solely on the despatches of the victorious generals. I readily recognize the essential part played in the development of science by persons of genius and deep insight, but the army of honest toilers has its role as well. We too are privileged to share, even if often at a distance and only vicariously, in those disclosure moments when a new pattern of understanding is grasped for the first time. Such occasions are times of shared wonder within the whole of the research community.

There was an easy way to organize the material for this second particle physics book. The community had for many years had a regular series of international town meetings, attended by a majority of the most active physicists, at which the current state of the art was presented and assessed. Initially, these conferences took place every year, changing later to become biennial as the pressure of other activities filled up the calendar. The meetings were called 'Rochester Conferences', after the North American university that initially had organized and hosted them before they became internationally nomadic, moving from hemisphere to hemisphere. Re-reading the proceedings of the Rochester Conferences gave one a series of snapshots of where the subject had been on each occasion and who were then being regarded as the principal movers and shakers. I based my book chapter by chapter on the conferences, and I gave it what I now see was probably an unduly gnomic title, *Rochester Roundabout* (1989). (I should have chosen something like *Discovering Quarks.*) The details involved in this sequential treatment inevitably made it a somewhat more demanding book for the non-professional reader than *Particle Play* had been. *Rochester Roundabout* sold moderately well, but I have to confess that I believe that it deserved a bit more attention than it actually seemed to receive. It is not my most important book, but I consider it to be the book that I have written that comes nearest to achieving what I had in mind in setting out to write it.

In is now time to narrow the focus onto my personal contributions to theoretical particle physics. They lay on the more mathematical side of the subject and the work had three principal phases. The first was concerned with analysing the mathematical properties that it was hoped would provide the foundations of S-matrix theory. The critical question was to determine what mathematicians call the 'singularity structure' of the physically relevant expressions involved (scattering amplitudes). Mathematical entities cannot be too well behaved if they are to be interesting. They have to have singularities, points where their behaviour becomes less smooth and generally agreeable than it is elsewhere. The only entity totally free from singularities is a boring constant. A great Russian theoretical physicist, Lev Landau, had written down some intuitively appealing equations that he claimed specified all the singularities associated with the S-matrix. There were two questions to be addressed: one was simply to ask whether the 'Landau singularities' were correct (he himself had not presented an argument in a form that a mathematician would acknowledge as convincing); and then what would the implications be for the actual complex properties of scattering amplitudes if this were so. A group of us in Cambridge devoted a lot of effort to answering these questions. The first major result was to show that the Landau singularities were indeed properties of Feynman integrals – in other words, that they emerged if you tried to solve the physics in a particular approximate way. I was then able to go on to show that they were general properties of S-matrix amplitudes. So far, so good, but detailed investigations then revealed that the mathematical structure actually flowing from these results was much more intricate than it had been hoped would prove to be the case. We also showed that in fact there was a further class of singularities that even Landau had not thought of. Several years of effort had produced a rather mixed result. Many intrinsic properties of relativistic quantum theory had been established that are necessary mathematical features of any fundamental theory. However, the delicate complexity of what had been discovered made it very difficult to extract many results in a form that was of direct physical usefulness. It turned out to be a kind of pyrrhic victory.

The next phase of my research involved studying the behaviour of scattering amplitudes at very high energies. In physics, extremity often produces simplicity, so that behaviour in a regime where some physical variable such as energy is large compared with the natural scales involved, may prove much easier to analyse than is the case for more moderate circumstances. An Italian physicist, Tullio Regge, had suggested that this might be the case for high energy particle scattering, proposing a particular form that this simplicity might take. However, his argument was based on using a model (technically, non-relativistic potential theory) that was not a fully adequate account of what was the actual (relativistic) case that needed to be considered. Using Feynman integrals as a fully relativistic model, I was able to confirm and extend Regge's conjecture, and elucidate some quite tricky details of the theory, which indeed proved to be more complicated than the simple potential model had suggested.

The third and final phase of research concentrated on deep inelastic scattering. As we have already noted, this is a regime of even greater extremity, since in it both energy and momentum transfer are large. A group of us in Cambridge did a lot of work in this area, using both Feynman integrals and other, more general models. We were able to provide some useful theoretical input into the interpretation of experimental results in the deep inelastic limit, work that played a contributory role in establishing the quark theory of matter.

A great deal of my research was done in collaboration with other members of the particle physics group in DAMTP. In particular, I wrote many papers with Peter Landshoff. He had been one of the first of my Cambridge research students, but he soon became a colleague working on at least equal terms. I owe a great debt of gratitude to Peter and to my other collaborators, who enabled me to do a lot more interesting physics than I would ever have been able to do simply on my own.

While research in science is deeply satisfying for its own sake, it is only natural that people also hope to receive some recognition from others of the contributions that they have made. The highly technical nature of scientific discourse means that this will have to come principally from one's peers in the subject. There are, of course, grand international awards, such as the Nobel Prize, but in science it is not hard to see roughly where one is in the pecking order, and for almost all of us there is the clear realization that there can be no expectation of such a great honour. For those of British Commonwealth nationality, however, there is a desirable award, some notches down on the intellectual scale from Nobel eminence but still representing a gratifying degree of professional attainment, namely election as a Fellow of the Royal Society. When I became a Cambridge professor in 1968, most of my scientific colleagues in the professoriate were FRSs, and I naturally hoped that I might join them in the not-too-distant future. In actual fact, it took somewhat longer for this to happen than I had hoped, for it was not until 1974 that I attained this recognition. (It is possible that matters were hindered by a degree of factionalism then present in the UK particle physics community – it is always easier to prevent someone being elected than to get someone in.) I was very pleased and relieved when the day did come for me to sign the Royal Society's Charter Book – a single volume, rebound from time to time, which contains the signatures of all the Fellows from the Society's foundation in 1660 onwards. I believe myself to be a person who, while not indifferent to awards, is not usually obsessed by them, but election to the Royal (as its Fellows tend to call the Society) was certainly something I longed for. I wrote a book about science in a wider human context (*Beyond Science*, 1996), in which I had to confess

> that the ambition to be an FRS was a potent and disturbing element in my scientific life for a good number of years. If you had put to me some curious scheme by which my election would have been assisted by the murder of my grandmother, I would certainly have declined, but there would have been a perceptible pause for mental struggle before I did so.

I am grateful for all that my membership of the particle physics community gave me. That community was a kind of international intellectual village where, after a few years of Rochester Conferences and other activities, you came to know to some degree most of the people in the business. When I left active research in theoretical physics, this communal academic life was one of the things that I missed the most. Nevertheless, despite the pleasures of life among the particle theorists, the time did come for departure. From the perspective of my Christian faith I had regarded it as having been part of my vocation to use such talents as I had for research. Generally speaking, it seems to me that one should endeavour to use whatever gifts that one seems to have been given. Yet in these mathematically based subjects you do not get better as you get older. Somehow one needs mental agility more than accumulated experience, and it becomes progressively harder for an old dog to learn new tricks. It is unlikely that most people do their best work before they are 25, but most do before they are 45. I had seen some of my senior and respected colleagues in the subject appear to find life less satisfying as the action moved away from them. I had long thought that I would not allow this to be my fate. Moreover, I was the senior member of a large and talented group of researchers in Cambridge who deserved the best leadership available. As the 1970s drew to a close, the Standard Model had been established and particle theory was beginning to move in new directions, such as string theory, that were both highly speculative and which called for different kinds of mathematics from that familiar to me. I came to the conclusion that it was time for a change. I always want to emphasize that I did not leave physics because I was in any way disillusioned with the subject. I retain a deep respect for my old subject and a lively interest in its progress. I simply felt that I had done my little bit for particle theory and the time had come to do something else.

9

Change

―――◦―――

By 1977, the year of my forty-seventh birthday, it seemed that the appropriate time had indeed arrived for me to start to consider future possibilities in a serious and realistic fashion. I suppose that one quite conventional move might have been in the direction of the higher flights of academic administration. I had served a four-year term on the General Board, Cambridge University's central body for formulating academic policy; I was a member of the Science Research Council, a national body in charge of a great deal of research funding; I was about to become the Chairman of SRC's Nuclear Physics Board. One way or another, I had accumulated quite a lot of experience of academic policy-making. No university had actually asked me if I would like to be its Vice-Chancellor, but such a position would not have seemed an outlandish possibility if my inclinations had veered in that direction. However, as I considered my future, praying about it and talking with Ruth, my mind turned in the quite different direction of seeking to enter the ordained ministry of the Church of England.

The most fundamental reason for thinking about such an unconventional move was simply that Christianity has always been central to my life. Therefore, becoming a minister of word and sacrament would be a privileged vocation that held out the possibility of deep satisfaction. I had also had a number of experiences that I can now see retrospectively to have been steps encouraging me to look towards the priesthood.

*Happy at the thought of
impending change*

One such step was learning something about the value of silence and meditative prayer. In Trinity, the Chaplains once a year organized a College retreat at the beginning of the Easter vacation. I was a Fellow deeply involved in Chapel life, and I had thought occasionally about the possibility of joining the party going on retreat. For a while I was deterred by learning that, apart from the times of worship, the whole proceedings were conducted in silence. With all the natural talkativeness of a don, I found this thought unappealing. However, one year I decided to give it a try, and I soon learned how positive is the experience of silence, and how genuinely related you become to the others who are sharing that silence with you. Since then I have tried to give silence and stillness a role in my life, valuing particularly opportunities to spend a few silent days in a religious House, in the course of which one can really begin to enter into the inner space that silence opens up.

Another formative experience was becoming a lay reader. One day, Michael Rees, the Vicar of Holy Trinity, asked me whether I had ever considered this possibility, which would involve some occasional preaching and the leading of non-eucharistic worship. I had not, but thinking about it I felt attracted, partly no doubt because it appealed to the pedagogic side of me, though I soon came to realize that preaching is quite different from lecturing. You are addressing more than just the minds of your listeners. Nowadays, readers in the Church of England have to undergo a quite demanding training programme of part-time study, extending over two years or so. In my time, however, things were much more informal, perhaps particularly if you were an academic. I had an agreeable interview with the Diocesan Warden of Readers, who asked me to write two or three specimen sermons. This I did while on a visit to Geneva to work at CERN. Apparently these draft sermons were satisfactory, and I was soon licensed and entitled to wear the cassock, surplice and characteristic blue scarf that is the ecclesiastical dress of a reader. There was not a great deal for me to do at Holy Trinity, as it turned out, for in term time the pulpit there tended to be occupied by a succession of guest preachers, but I was able to go out into the country from time to time to take Evensong in a village church. I enjoyed these experiences, but there was some degree of frustration in not being able to exercise a eucharistic ministry. I believe that the Church celebrates the Eucharist in direct obedience to the command of its risen Lord, who is present with the gathered worshippers, and the sacramental life has been a mainstay of my own Christian pilgrimage.

A third formative experience resulted from the arrival of a family, the Hutchisons, who came to live near us and whose four children overlapped in age with ours. They too worshipped at Holy Trinity, and Eric, the father, proved to be a very remarkable man. He had served in the Canadian Navy during the war, was eventually ordained and had worked for a while in East Africa teaching theology. Now he had come to Cambridge, both for further study and to train and practise as a Jungian psychotherapist. Eric continued to exercise his priestly ministry on a non-stipendiary basis, as part of which he had started a neighbourhood Bible study group which met in the Hutchisons' home. Ruth joined this group and after about a year she told me that it was proving so stimulating and helpful an experience that I too ought to consider joining. I was not very anxious to take on further regular commitments, but I decided nevertheless to try it out. The result was several years of regular attendance by both of us, which turned out to be very significant in the development of our Christian lives. Eric had a great gift for teaching. The group was fairly diverse in personalities and educational backgrounds, but he was able to make the meetings ones in which all participated and from which all gained insight. My years in the group taught me much and opened my eyes to the way in which scripture may be used truly to expand one's understanding, rather than narrowing it. Eric's own theology was Barthian in tone, following the emphasis laid by Karl Barth, arguably the most influential theologian of the twentieth century, on the unique power of the Word of God in Jesus Christ, considered by Barth to be the sole fundamental source of knowledge of the divine nature and will for humanity. I have not become quite as Barthian as Eric, for he was not the kind of teacher who tries to impose his views on others, but I owe him an immense debt of gratitude for those years of Bible study under his guidance.

I also owe a second debt to Eric, for I not only learned more about God from him, but I also learned more about myself. His Jungian skills and insights helped me personally to explore a little of the riches that lie in the depths of the unconscious psyche.

These experiences were certainly very helpful to me in shaping my thoughts about a change of direction towards the priesthood. Of course, the decision was not one for me alone, for it had to be a joint decision arrived at with Ruth. She had married me when I was a young academic, and I could not simply tell her one day that all that was about to change abruptly. We talked and prayed about the future, and I also sought advice from a very small number of wise close friends, including Eric. When eventually the decision had been made and the news became public, I had one or two interviews with media people about what had been happening. I think that the interviewers were rather hoping for a dramatic, Damascus road, story, but in the end it all turned out to be much lower key than that. I must admit that I had thought that perhaps it would all climax in something like Ruth and I going off for a few days' retreat in some Religious House before reaching the final decision. In fact, even that did not prove necessary. In a quiet way, and fortunately in both our minds, over a period of a few months the idea of my seeking ordination seemed clearly to be the right way ahead. The decision was made easier by the fact that our children were growing up and going off to university, allowing their parents to gain greater room for manoeuvre in their own lives without the danger of failing to honour family obligations. Ruth herself was soon to take advantage of this. She now had the opportunity to take up a job again. For her too, this would mean a significant change, for instead of returning to statistics she decided to train to become a state-registered nurse. Soon she was successfully following the demanding course of training required for her new vocation, at the same time as I was preparing for the priesthood.

As far as my own middle-aged adventure was concerned, the next step was to contact the church authorities who would have to decide whether I had a true calling to the ministry. I went to see the Diocesan Director of Ordinands, John Byrom, a deeply spiritual man who quite unselfconsciously had the manifest air of someone who lived closely in the presence of God. He opened our conversation by asking whether it would not be a suitable vocation for me to remain as a lay Christian witness working in the academic world. I explained why I believed this was no longer my calling, and John accepted what I had to say. I then had to go to a selection conference organized by ACCM (the Advisory Council for the Church's Ministry), at which a dozen or so prospective ordinands would spend three days in prayer, group activities and individual interviews with a body of selectors, as an exercise in discernment into the possibility of their being called to the ordained ministry.

I arrived at the Sheffield Diocesan Retreat House where my conference was to be held, to find a purple-shirted figure seated on the lawn under the shade of a cedar tree, drinking tea out of a silver teapot – a very Anglican scene. I felt I ought to go over and introduce myself. 'I'm called Bishop,' he said. I supposed that this must mean that selectors operated anonymously, being known only by their office. It was only later that I learned that he was Bishop Bishop. As is inevitable in any selection process, different people will evaluate their experiences differently, partly depending on the verdicts, which in this case could be 'Yes', 'No' or 'Wait a while'. I was accepted, but I do not think that positive result is the only reason why I am grateful to ACCM. It was helpful to talk things over with experienced people who had no prior connection with you, and I was glad that there was no sign at all of their being over-impressed by a Cambridge professor who was an FRS. Any process of significant change will have its ups and downs, and there will be moments in which you wonder exactly what is happening to you and what you have let yourself in for. At such times, it was encouraging to remember that careful thought had been given by others to the wisdom and appropriateness of the move that you were making.

Up to the time of the selection conference, my thoughts and intentions had been known to only a very few people, but as soon as I knew that I was accepted for training, it became necessary to share my plans more widely. First to be told, of course, were our children. One Sunday they were all at home for lunch and after the meal I told them what was going to happen, including that in due course we would have to move out of our family home in Rutherford Road to a smaller house elsewhere in Cambridge. Isobel immediately said that she had sensed for some time that something was going on, but she had not guessed what it was. The child most affected was Michael, since he was still at school and living at home all the year round. Understandably he needed a little time to adjust fully to the unexpected news. Rather touchingly, he told me that he had been proud to have a professor as a father and was sorry that was going to change. However, the whole family soon accepted the news and were supportive of me. Being believers, they could understand my motivation.

The next people to be told were my colleagues in our research group. We senior staff were having a meeting to fix postdoctoral positions for the following year when, after the business was settled, I said, 'Don't go yet, I have something else to tell you.' I remember vividly the astonished silence that followed my announcement. It was broken by Peter Landshoff. He is not a religious person, but he said to me that, while he had not foreseen what I was going to do, if he had been told I was leaving physics, he would have guessed what I had chosen to do next. I found that remark helpful and supportive, and I was grateful for the generally accepting response that I received from colleagues in DAMTP. At the time Steven Weinberg, a Nobel Laureate in Physics and a staunch atheist, was a visitor to our group. I had the chance to tell him about my unconventional move when he and his wife were having dinner with us at our home. Steve is the sort of atheist who seems rather to like to talk about God and, while he could not share my convictions, he too was not inclined to be dismissive of my intentions.

Of course, I was not going to leave the Department immediately, as I had to wind up my academic affairs in a responsible fashion. I could not just say to my research students, 'Cheerio – and I hope you get a PhD.' There was a period of about 18 months in which it was known that I was leaving but I had not yet left. News of my unusual decision had spread quite rapidly in the village gossip of the particle physics community. As a result, I had a number of interesting conversations over a cup of coffee in some laboratory canteen, in which friends asked me what was I really up to. Mostly they were not so much concerned with my decision to enter the ministry, as with exploring why I had a clear commitment to the Christian faith. In half an hour or so's chat it was not possible to do more than indicate a little of why the figure of Jesus Christ is so important to me (any more than I could in half an hour have given a non-scientific colleague an adequate account of why I believed in quarks and gluons).

As I thought about these conversations, there formed in my mind what I would have liked to have said if I had been given several hours in which to do so. Eventually, this led me to write my first book about science and religion, a short account of how I need, and feel able, to take both scientific insight and Christian insight with the utmost seriousness. To this slim volume I gave the rather grandiose title *The Way the World Is* (1983). I chose that title to indicate that I believe that the truthful and careful exploration of reality, seeking well-motivated understanding, is a common feature of both science and religion, even though they are concerned with very different dimensions of reality. Lots of things were to change for me as I trained for ordination and became a clergyman, but one thing did not change at all between the two halves of my adult life, for both have been concerned with the search for truth.

10

Westcott

In 1979 I resigned my Chair in order to start training for the ministry. Ruth started her nursing training at the same time, travelling each day to the West Suffolk Hospital at Bury St Edmunds, since Addenbrookes, the large District General Hospital in Cambridge, would not accept student nurses over the age of 40 and by then she was 48. Michael was still at the Leys, Isobel was starting at Oxford, and Peter would soon be in gainful employment. We had moved to a small house in Belvoir Road, nearer to Westcott House where I was to train. Each morning at about 7.15 I cycled over to Westcott for the Morning Office, crossing the Cam by the Fort St George bridge. My feeling of self-satisfaction at an early start was somewhat diminished by the sight of College eights returning from their practice rowing. Words of St Paul crossed my mind: 'They do it to receive a perishable crown, but we an imperishable' (1 Corinthians 9.25, NASB).

Our family need to remain living in Cambridge for a little longer had meant that my choice of theological college had to be between the two local Anglican seminaries, Westcott House and Ridley Hall, the former standing in a liberal catholic tradition, the latter in a moderate evangelical tradition. They were both part of the Cambridge Theological Federation, which also included the Methodist seminary of Wesley House and the United Reformed seminary of Westminster College. (Later the Federation expanded to include additional constituent institutions.) This ecumenical dimension to Christian studies was a valuable asset, giving one the opportunity to get to know non-Anglican traditions, even if federal relations were a bit creaky at times. Each term one ate one meal a week at another House, and on Sundays there was a Federation Eucharist taken in turn by clergy from each of the seminaries. Lectures were also mostly shared, though the more delicate matter of doctrine was taught separately in each House.

I knew Ridley very well, for I had been a lay member of its Council for several years. I particularly respected its Principal, Keith Sutton, later Bishop of Lichfield, with whom I had some valuable talks about what lay ahead for me. Keith said to me one day that I ought to start reading some serious theology by way of preparation, and he suggested that I should begin with *The Crucified God*, a book written by a leading German Protestant theologian, Jürgen Moltmann. I was bowled over by the book's powerful exposition of the cross of Christ, understood as true divine participation in the suffering of the world. For Moltmann, the Christian God is not simply a compassionate spectator of the travail of creation, but a fellow-sufferer who knows pain and rejection from the inside. Here is the most profound Christian response to the deep problem of evil and suffering, the difficulty that surely holds more people back from religious belief than any other, and which continues to trouble and challenge those of us who are believers. The insight of the crucified God is at the heart of my own Christian belief, and indeed of the possibility of that belief. Later I was to go on to read all of Moltmann's major writings, and he has been the contemporary theologian who has helped and influenced me the most. I have subsequently had the privilege of getting to know him personally.

Despite my connections with Ridley, I decided that I would apply to go to Westcott. I felt that I knew the tradition that Ridley represented pretty well and that it would broaden my experience to do my training in a somewhat different setting. I think the choice was a wise one. Westcott affirmed my growing recognition of the centrality of the sacramental life. Worshipping day by day in its simple but beautiful chapel also taught me what I believe was the most important lesson of my training, the value of the Daily Office, that regular recitation of Morning and Evening Prayer which brings with it the connected reading of scripture and a continuous engagement with the spiritual force of the Psalms as they are read 'in course' (that is, in sequence). The use of psalmody has been going on for 2,500 years, from the time of the Second Temple in Jerusalem to the present day. What gives the Psalms a particular force is, I believe, their honesty. They express a much wider range of religious emotion than you will find in any hymn book, ranging from expressions of deep trust in the faithfulness of God to frank cries of anger and protest. (Psalm 44 even tells God to wake up and take notice of what is happening.)

During my time at Westcott, an icon was commissioned for the chapel, painted in traditional style by a modern icon painter. It portrays Christ holding an open book, and as its completion came near we were asked as a community to say what verse we would wish to be inscribed on the book. Consultation led to unanimous agreement to ask for 'You have not chosen me, but I have chosen you' (John 15.16). The painter was deeply moved when told of this choice, for she had had just that verse in her mind while she prayerfully painted the icon. I have a photograph of the icon in my study and I repeat those words each day.

In terms of the spiritual life, I am a pretty humdrum Christian. I have not had any tremendous experiences of numinous encounter or mystical union, but the exercise of my Christian discipleship centres on regular worship, prayer, witness and service. The Daily Office suits my sort of spirituality very well, providing a framework for each day and an observance whose regularity is an expression of my commitment to the cause of God and Christ.

I enjoyed my two years at Westcott very much. I was the oldest person in the House, senior in age if not in status to the Principal, Mark Santer, later Bishop of Birmingham. Most of my fellow students were in their later twenties and they were a varied and talented bunch. I enjoyed their friendly companionship, even if at times, as someone who had been married for about 25 years and had helped to bring up three children, I occasionally felt rather wise and experienced.

There were many things that I needed to learn from the lectures that

I attended. The courses I enjoyed the most were in biblical studies. If you are a scientist, your instinct on entering a new field is to look first at the basic phenomena that you will have to take into account and which will shape your thinking. For the student of Christian theology this implies a particular concern with the study of the New Testament. I had prepared myself for this by teaching myself elementary New Testament Greek, as a blameless evening occupation while I was on my own on a last extended visit to CERN. I knew that I did not have the linguistic skills to become a proper New Testament scholar, but I wanted to learn as much as I could. I still read as many books on New Testament theology as possible, and if a fairy godmother were to offer me one magic wish I would ask to become a New Testament expert (with being an organist as the default choice in this fantasy exercise).

Of course, one cannot properly understand the New Testament without an understanding of its roots in the Hebrew Bible, and I was taught Old Testament, and (voluntary) Hebrew, by Mary Tanner. We became good friends and have remained in touch after she left the House to return to being an important figure in national and international ecumenical relations. My principal regret about the academic side of my Westcott experience was that I did not go in my first year to the doctrine course, an option that I could have exercised, but did not because the general recommendation was that one took this course in one's second year after a concentration on biblical studies in the first year. Thereby I missed the opportunity to sit at the feet of Rowan Williams, now Archbishop of Canterbury and an insightful theologian from whom it would have been good to learn. By the time my second year came round, he had left Westcott for a post in the University.

Another aspect of our training was on the practical side. This involved a variety of activities. One was a social survey of church life in two fenland parishes that had been at enmity since the Civil War, but which were now having to share the same vicar. This bird's-eye view of parochial life demonstrated, if one needed the lesson, that life in the Christian fold is not always one of unlimited harmony and light. A major activity in pastoral training was regular hospital visiting. I was successively assigned to two wards in Addenbrookes, the first with leukaemia patients, the second with anorexics. In both of these wards people were undergoing extreme experiences. Often one could do no more than be with them, listening and silently sharing something of their situation. There was one particular thing, however, that one could do for the anorexics, who mostly had been sectioned and were in hospital against their will and whose lives were closely circumscribed. This was simply to go away when they told you that they had had enough of you, something that they could say to practically nobody else.

It was inevitable to pray for all these patients when one got home, but I did not suppose that all whom I visited would miraculously be cured. So what was one doing when one prayed? I concluded that what I was seeking was to help bring them and their suffering into the presence of God. There was no magic word or magic action that would make everything all right, but there was a modest kind of tacit and respectful alongsideness that could be offered, both through presence and through prayer. Sometimes one even knew what to do. One afternoon I encountered in a corridor a woman who was very upset. Her husband appeared to be dying in a particularly distressful way and she had found that she just could not bear to sit and watch this happening. Just to take her hand, lead her back and sit with her at the bedside until her husband came out of his distress (he did not die until many weeks later) was what needed to be done.

Another term I went once a week to lend a hand with children who have multiple handicaps living in a special home. I learned two things from this experience. One was to admire the patience and love of the staff, who devoted much time and skill to achieving what, in a coldly objective way, might have seemed to be small gains – helping a child to tell blue from red, for example – but which were real gifts to these young people. The second thing was to recognize immediately and intuitively that, however confined and bound some of these children were by their circumstances, there could not for a moment be a doubt that they were persons, with all the worth and respect that attaches to that.

The practical side of training also involved some ecclesiastical kinds of experience: classes in preaching; taking turns at leading the Office and serving at the Eucharist; practising the actions for baptism on a real baby, generously lent by his parents for this purpose. The one thing we were never taught was how to sing, despite the demands that the liturgy can make on clergy for minor amounts of solo performance. It was simply assumed, incorrectly in my case, that anyone could do this just by nature.

It was odd becoming a student again after so many years as a university teacher. I was very used to standing up and talking for an hour, but it was much more difficult to listen to someone else for that length of time. However good the lecture might be, after about 45 minutes I often began to be restless and wonder when it was going to finish. However, if student life began to pall, I could always find relief, for I was leading a double life. Although I had quit my university professorship, I remained a Fellow of Trinity – and the College, with great generosity, allowed me to earn a living as a part-time supervisor in mathematical physics. This enabled me to work my way through Westcott without becoming a charge on church funds for fees or living expenses. It also enabled me to walk a few hundred yards up Jesus Lane from Westcott and turn into a don. The occasional High Table meal was a welcome relief from theological college food. At that time Westcott had given up having its own kitchens and we all ate over the road at Wesley House. This was something of a problem on such occasions as end-of-term, pre-Christmas festivities, for the Methodist rules of Wesley did not permit the consumption of alcohol on the premises.

Student food was an issue that nearly turned me into a student rebel. The rule at Westcott was that one had to purchase a complete set of meals for the term and there was no financial rebate if you did not eat them all. The only recompense offered for unconsumed meals was being given credit for them against any charges there might be for a guest that you had brought in. This was of no use to me. Ruth and Michael were both eating institutional food during the week, so more of it under Westcott auspices scarcely seemed an attractive prospect for them. Any academic friends I wanted to entertain could be taken to Trinity. I joined with a few other married students at Westcott to start a campaign to get the rules changed so that one at least got a rebate for the food not actually eaten. (We recognized that requiring a continuing contribution to overheads was not unreasonable.) There were arguments at Monday evening House Meetings, but the authorities simply held firm and said no. I burned with indignation. I could see that the only way in which we might get anywhere was some form of direct action (a fee-strike?). However, I was sufficiently gentlemanly, and had a sufficiently strong fellow-feeling still for those in academic authority, to realize that even to suggest this to my fellow agitators would be a kind of treason of the clerks, so in the end we simply acquiesced in the *status quo*.

My two years at Westcott House were a good time for me. I hope this account succeeds in reflecting the happiness of that transitional period in my life. I do not say that there were never times when I wondered what I was up to, and then it was helpful to recall the recognition of my vocation that I had been given at my ACCM selection conference. At the end of our two years together, my contemporaries and I parted with much affection and gratitude for the life that we had lived together. The next step for all of us was ordination as a deacon, which for each of us would take place in the cathedral of the particular diocese in which we were to serve. For a Cambridge resident like me this was Ely, for my life had to continue beside the Cam for one more year. Training to become a nurse takes three years (you have to be careful with people whose mistakes might be visible in this life), rather than the two years required of a 'mature' (i.e. over 30) candidate for orders, and so Belvoir Road was to remain our home a little longer.

11

Curate

———⟫•◦•⟪———

English professional life has a long tradition of learning through practical experience on the job. Accountants and lawyers are articled to firms, junior doctors work in hospitals as house officers. Although this apprenticeship approach has been somewhat eroded recently by an increasing tendency to emphasize the role of academic paper qualifications, it has not at all diminished in that other 'learned profession', the ordained ministry of the Church of England. It is not possible to be ordained on spec, as it were, for one must be ordained to what is called a 'title', normally a curacy that will be held for three years in a specific parish under the practical and spiritual supervision of the vicar.

For reasons already explained, I had to spend the first year of my title in Cambridge, and so it was arranged that I should be a part-time, non-stipendiary curate in the parish in which we lived, St Andrew's, Chesterton. Accordingly, I was ordained deacon in Ely Cathedral at the end of June 1981 by Peter Walker, the Diocesan Bishop. About ten other deacons were being ordained at the same time and we spent a few days beforehand in retreat at Bishop Woodford House. The retreat was led by an experienced parish priest from the diocese. The only thing that I now remember from what he said is that, while he affirmed that saying the Office regularly was a very important duty, he also emphasized that the exact times at which one did so were matters of simple convenience in relation to the other activities of the day, and one should not get too rigid about it. He revealed that he often said the Evening Office imme-diately after lunch, since that frequently fitted best with the other things he had to do. It may seem rather a trivial point, but I found this kind of commonsense stance a helpful example in the years ahead.

When ordination Sunday arrived, we had only to step across the road to the Cathedral. We carried over our arms our white stoles, which after the bishop had laid hands on us in the name of the God and the Church, we would wear 'deaconwise', that is, over the left shoulder and tied on the right at the waist. This was the liturgically significant dress signal of the new status that we had been given but, such is the power of general culture, I believe that another sartorial gesture affected most of us more strongly at the time. We had been told that we should wear our clerical collars for the first time as we went to the ordination service. I detected in myself and in others a distinct tendency to postpone this act until the last possible moment. Somehow the adoption of this clerical dress code (in fact, only invented in the nineteenth century and with nothing like the venerable history of the stole) seemed at the time the most powerful symbol of irreversible change.

During my part-time deacon's year, my duties at St Andrew's were modest. I spent one afternoon a week in parish visiting and, of course, I participated in the Sunday services, preaching regularly and assisting at Holy Communion, though the actual act of celebrating the sacrament was a privilege reserved to priests. I particularly enjoyed preaching, as I still do. I am an expository preacher rather than an exhortatory one, my aim being to help people understand something more about the scrip-ture passages set for the day and then largely leaving the application to the individual conscience and understanding. Partly, no doubt, this approach owes something to my academic background, but it is also related to my concept of the role of liturgy. One of its great values, I believe, is to provide a spiritually serious setting in the presence of God, but normally to refrain from imposing a single mood. On any Sunday in church there will be people in the congregation who are happy and grateful, and those who are sad and perplexed. The framework of scrip-ture and psalmody is wide enough to furnish a place in which all can find a home that day. I also value the rhythm of the Church's year that inexorably presents to us in sequence the great truths of the faith to be thought of and spoken about, and I am grateful for the discipline of the lectionary that prescribes for the preacher the texts to be tackled each Sunday, thus avoiding the trap of being caught in mere personal preference.

The vicar of St Andrew's was John Carré, a priest coming to the end of his full-time ministry who had, perhaps, become a little tired by then by the wear and tear of parish life, but who was devout and faithful in a way that I admired. We said the Office in church each morning, together with Margaret, a parishioner who was very faithful in this observance. St Andrew's had a strong musical tradition, a great asset for worship since music can reach such great depths within us. At times, such as a special Festal Evensong, this musicality made modest but challenging demands on John or me. Finally, from time to time I did 'crem duty'. At that time the Cambridge churches had acquiesced in a rota system by which most funerals at the local crematorium were taken by the duty clergyman of the day. This suited the funeral directors, but it was disastrous pastorally, as one was mostly faced with taking the funerals of people whom one did not know for families one had not met. The cortège would arrive and the funeral director in a hasty whisper would say something such as, 'Seventy-three; cancer', and you had to do the best you could with that. I am glad to say that this system has long ceased in Cambridge.

Later in my parish ministry, the funerals that I took were on a much more personal basis. One had visited the family beforehand and had been able to learn something about the deceased that one could use in the address. It may seem odd to say so, but when eventually I became an academic clergyman, and consequently only very occasionally took funerals, I missed this form of ministry. It gave you the privilege of being with people at a significant and often difficult moment in their lives. The Christian hope of a destiny beyond death, given us by the everlasting faithfulness of God manifested in the resurrection of Christ, is a message that one can seek to share to the extent that you judge the bereaved are capable of hearing it at that time.

On the secular front, I was in my last year of teaching for Trinity. I also had a certain amount of time to spare, which I devoted partly to writing *The Way the World Is*, and partly to further academic study of theology, including attending some university courses. As my deacon's year drew to a close, the time approached for my ordination to the priesthood, an event to which I had been looking forward with eagerness, since I greatly valued the prospect of being given the privilege of presiding at the Eucharist on behalf of the gathered company of believers. The Dean of Chapel in Trinity at this time was John Robinson, erstwhile Bishop of Woolwich and the author of the celebrated theological best-seller, *Honest to God*. Peter Walker most kindly suggested to John and me that the ordination might be a personal occasion, taking place in Trinity Chapel on Trinity Sunday, with John as the ordaining bishop under letters dimissory (authorization) from the Bishop of Ely. We were both delighted at this prospect, which duly took place as planned. On such an occasion, priests can join with the bishop in laying hands on the ordinand. It was, therefore, possible for me to invite some friends to do this for me, including the distinguished patristic scholar Henry Chadwick, and my friend Eric Hutchison, who preached the sermon.

It was a very happy day for me, for my family and, I believe, for the Christian community in Trinity. I was particularly glad to have John Robinson as my ordaining bishop, as we had become good friends during his time in College. I loved John for his humanity and faithfulness. He was a man of deep Christian commitment, and the caricature of him as someone on the outskirts of the faith was a mere media image, though admittedly one not always obviously contradicted by the headline-catching way in which he sometimes chose to express himself. John was, in fact, the most unreconciled mixture of the instinctively traditional (he had been born in the Close at Canterbury) and the intuitively radical that I have ever encountered. Often one could see him change gear between the two in the course of a single conversation. John was also capable of uttering outrageous remarks without batting an eyelid, or noticing that he had done so. He was sitting next to me at lunch on the High Table one day, and in the course of our conversation (about what I cannot now remember), he turned to me and said, 'A Protestant rationalist like you would not understand that.' I boiled with indignation at this totally unjustified characterization, but John obviously had no idea that he had vexed me.

It is possible that I was the last priest that John ordained, for soon after I had left Cambridge he was diagnosed as having an inoperable cancer. All of us who were his friends, and many of those who had been opposed to him in some way before, greatly admired the Christian hope and fortitude with which he, and his wife Ruth, lived those last six months. The last sermon that John preached in Chapel was a courageous discourse, 'On living with cancer', that moved all who heard it, together with those of us who read it afterwards.

Oddly enough, my deacon's year was the time when I felt most qualms about my change of life. They were not induced by my experiences as a tyro clergyman, but they were probably the result of two factors. One was that, for that year I had more leisure time in which to reflect on what was happening to me. I became more aware of the discontinuities involved in the move from physicist to parson. Of course, there were continuities also, the most important of which, as I have already said, was that in both science and religion the issue of truth is paramount, even if the kinds of truth involved are very different. In the one case it is truth about the impersonal physical world open to our scientific manipulation and experimental interrogation; in the other case it is truth about the transpersonal reality of God, the One who is only fittingly to be encountered with awe and worship and obedience. Nevertheless, the fact of the matter was that I had moved from being an established expert to being in the position of one who had much that he still needed to learn.

The other factor at work was a realization of how different the worlds of academy and church are from each other. I had acquired some familiarity with, and standing in, the former, but now I had slid down a snake to land myself as a novice member of a quite different social community. The contrast between the two worlds can be illustrated by the relevant issue of how one actually goes about finding a job. Of course, in both worlds there are informal networks of connection that operate to ensure that some people's names are drawn to the attention of those with power to appoint. Yet in university life, almost all jobs are advertised and one can always try one's luck by applying. At the very least, one knows what possibilities are in principle available. As far as church positions are concerned, even today some are not advertised and what actually happens will often depend upon the (to some extent adventitious) knowledge acquired by bishops, archdeacons and the like. Often this system works very well, and the degree of personal acquaintance involved can result in someone being fitted into just the position that will make good use of their individual talents and experience. However, one can also come across people who seem to have been washed up on what for them is some alien shore, with little expectation of being floated off on an incoming episcopal tide.

I should make it clear that these reservations about how the Church uses its human resources arise from general reflection and not from any particularly unfortunate experience on my part. As it has turned out, I have had no grounds for personal complaint about the authorities (or, perhaps, for exceptional gratitude either), but that this would be so was not at all obvious as my deacon's year drew to a close. I simply knew that after my priesting, after Ruth's qualifying as a nurse, and after Michael's leaving school, the time had come to leave Cambridge. My father had recently died in his early nineties, and I was anxious to find a position not too far from Wells where my mother, in her late eighties and with increasing eyesight problems, was still living. Training parishes tend to be in urban areas and so it was towards the diocese of Bristol that I turned my hopeful eye. I had an interview with David Isitt, the Canon in charge of novice curates. This lead to my first tentative encounter with a prospective parish, located in a socially upmarket area of the city, whose vicar was about my age. He rightly concluded – though I did not myself see this so clearly at the time – that what he actually wanted was a significantly younger curate who could deal with the youth club, certainly not my home territory. The next possibility was a wholly working-class parish in Bedminster (a southern part of Bristol), St Michael and All

St Michael and All Angels, Windmill Hill; the church in Bristol
where I served my full-time curacy

Angels, Windmill Hill. The vicar was Peter Chambers, a younger man than me and someone, I was encouraged to see from our first meeting, who would not be at all worried at the prospect of having an ex-Cambridge professor as a curate. The deal was done and soon we moved into the curate's house. With characteristic generosity and practical skill, Peter devoted a few days to building for me a large bookcase in my study, capable of accommodating, at least for the time being, my growing collection of books.

We enjoyed Windmill Hill. I felt I had come home by returning to the West Country of my youth, and Ruth and I made many friends in the congregation, including particularly Peter and his wife Joan. Ruth took a full-time nursing job at the Bristol General Hospital, to which she could cycle from where we lived. (She had hoped she might get a job at the local Hospice, but perhaps that was too much to expect for a nurse only recently qualified.) During the dozen or so years she was to spend working as a nurse, Ruth always took jobs on geriatric wards, preferring the hands-on nursing this required, hard work though this could be, to a more high-tech kind of activity at some remove from the individual patient. Michael was now an undergraduate at Trinity, needing to be ferried to and fro with a mound of equipment that included several varieties of clarinet and saxophone. I got down to the regular life of a novice parish priest.

I owe a great debt to Peter Chambers for his concern for me and his wise initiation into many aspects of pastoral care. Right at the start he told me that it was important for clergy to have a sustainable way of life and not to succumb to the temptation to attempt to justify themselves by overwork. (At clergy chapter meetings you would see people stagger in carrying diaries, it seemed as large as gospel books, no doubt intended to be testimonies to their unrelenting busyness.) Peter said that he aimed to work a 40-hour week, to which he added some 'voluntary' activity such as any church member might be willing to undertake. He was particularly keen on marriage preparation and later came to occupy for a while a national post with responsibilities in that area. I sat in on a few interviews and then tried my hand solo. I suppose that what I most wanted to convey in that setting was to give the couple an understanding that they would be making their vows to each other in the presence of God, that it belongs to our humanity to desire and to give the support of life-long love and fidelity, and that the greatest change that can come in one's life is when one starts a family.

My first experience of actually taking a wedding plunged me in at the deep end. It was a Saturday afternoon and the bride was due at 2.30. By three o'clock she had not appeared. The organist had been playing for half an hour, trying to keep the congregation from getting too restless. I knew that I had to stay essentially without limit, but I began to screw myself up to taking the decision to tell the organist that enough was enough and he could now go home if he wanted to. Just at that moment, the bride arrived, accompanied by her father who was swaying slightly and smelling strongly of whisky. I kept a stern eye on him during the ceremony to try to convey the message that we wanted no further trouble.

How effective this was I do not know, but once we had got going all went on to a satisfactory ending. Brides are quite often a little late, but I never again had so trying an experience.

Another 'occasional office' that fell to the parish priest was baptism, usually of young babies. One would visit the family beforehand for preparation. Often the television was on when you arrived and they would frequently simply turn off the sound. I felt I had to ask, as courteously as possible, for the set itself to be turned off, since otherwise people's eyes returned continually to the moving screen. Baptism is a sacrament making the recipient a member of Christ's Church, and it is certainly much more than giving the baby a name or even thanking God for the gift of a child. Great promises have to be made, and great truths affirmed, on the baby's behalf by parents and godparents. I felt that I had to explain as clearly as I could what was involved, and then trust that people responded with integrity to what they had been able to take in. Later I was to see something of the deep hurt caused by too rigorous a baptismal policy that could lead some people to feel that the Church was rejecting their baby. A measure of the grace and loving acceptance of God had to be reflected in these encounters with families who were seeking something which was often more than they could clearly express.

Early on in my Bristolian ministry, a neighbouring priest had said to me that in his opinion a lot of the life of a parish clergyman was simply 'bumming around' to see what happened and to try to be alert and responsive to what was going on. A good deal of my life at St Michael's was spent in this mode, particularly in the form of parish visiting. Our part of Bristol was Wills country, for until recently the tobacco firm had had a big local factory and many of the older parishioners had worked there. Whatever one might think of the tobacco industry generally, Wills were very good employers, organizing free summer outings for their pensioners and maintaining a welfare officer who paid regular visits to see how people were getting on. Windmill Hill was a very stable part of town, where people characteristically lived in the terrace house that mum and dad had bought for a few hundred pounds in the 1930s. This gave the area something of the character of a village, an ethos that I had not realized was possible within a big city. People would notice if the old lady opposite did not take in her milk one morning, and go across to check that she was all right. There was also a strongly localized feel about the place, so that people tended not to look very far afield. I remember early on going to visit an elderly lady. I asked her if she had a family and she told me that she had a married daughter. 'Does she live near?' I enquired. Her face fell. 'Oh no,' she replied, 'she lives in Whitchurch,' fully a mile and a half up the main road.

During my time in Bristol I had a very significant and, at the time, unwelcome experience. Suddenly, quite out of the blue, I became very seriously ill. It was so unexpected that at first it took a little while for me (and my doctor) to realize what was happening. Eventually I was admitted to the Bristol Royal Infirmary and after a week or so of unavailing medical treatment, it was decided that I must have an immediate emergency operation. Two things happened that day that were generous and encouraging gifts to me. As I was being got ready for the theatre, my physician, Dr Barry, asked me where my wife was. In fact, Ruth was in the Bristol Royal Infirmary that day, attending a course. On hearing this, Ralph Barry immediately went personally to tell her what was happening and to bring her out so that we were able to have a few words together before I was taken into the anaesthetic room. There my anaesthetist, just before she put me under, said to me, 'You have a wonderful surgeon.' That was just about the most encouraging message you could be given before a major operation.

The anaesthetist was right and I am very grateful for Mr Mortenson's skill. However, after the operation I felt very weak and debilitated. My whole world had closed in to my hospital bed and the drips that were keeping me alive. My attention was focused on those drips, as if they needed continual mental assistance to do their job properly. God seemed very far away and I could not manage to pray. Yet I was deeply conscious of being prayed for, by my family, by my church and by some Anglican nuns who had become friends of mine. This weight of vicarious prayer sustained me. Twice I had a kind of brief vision, or waking dream, in which I saw one of the sisters kneeling in prayer in the chapel at Tymawr, as I had so often seen them do. I was learning something of the communion of saints and the power of prayer.

Gradually strength returned and I was able to return home for a long convalescence. All did not go smoothly, for I had to return to hospital again to have an adhesion dealt with, and there was also a final tidying-up operation that was necessary, so altogether I had three bouts of abdominal surgery. I still return in my thoughts to that time of traumatic experience – and to the kindnesses and prayers that I was given. Afterwards, when I was back in the ministry and again visiting people who were gravely ill, I was able to understand more fully what was happening to them, and I believe that, consciously or subconsciously, they could recognize that I was not a total stranger to what they were going through.

I have twice mentioned some nuns who are my friends. They are the Sisters of the Society of the Sacred Cross, living a kind of Cistercian life in a convent outside Monmouth, not too far across the Severn Bridge from Bristol. It was during my curacy that I visited Tymawr for the first time and so our friendship began. Some years before, when the news of my impending change of life had become public, one of the Sisters, who had a maths degree from Cambridge and who had attended some of my lectures, listened to an interview with me on the radio. She wrote to me and we corresponded a little. When I came to Bristol, I naturally went to visit the Convent so that I could meet my correspondent, Sister Theresa, together with Reverend Mother and the other Sisters. In the wise way that nuns have, they set me to work helping with the potato harvest, a good way of playing myself in. Friendship soon grew between myself and the community and eventually I became a priest-associate of SSC, following a simple rule of prayerful relationship and sending them postcards when I am on my travels, since the Sisters live a largely stable life without much change of scene. Their home, Tymawr Convent, is my spiritual home too. I try to get there when I can, but it is not altogether easy from far-away Cambridge, and I am not as good at this as I would like to be.

The religious life of monks and nuns is a very important, but often hidden, dimension of the life of the Church. England is dotted with religious houses, many open for retreats by visitors, and all ceaselessly active centres of prayer. I am often pleased by the number of people I meet who turn out to be part in some way of the great web of prayer that centres on Tymawr. We who live in the world gain much from our friends in the cloister, but we should not suppose that the gifts that they give us are not costly to them. The religious life has its problems. Vocations these days seem to come slowly, and SSC is a community whose average age increases as its numbers drop. My friend Sister Theresa eventually left the Convent, becoming Pat again. It is a long while since we have seen each other face to face (she lived for many years in Shetland), but we manage still to keep in touch at Christmas time.

Peter Chambers left St Michael's during the second year of my curacy. My illness prevented my holding the fort for as much of the interregnum as had been planned, but I did get back in action before it became time to leave. By then my two years were drawing to a close and I needed to find out what I was to do next.

12

Vicar

While serving in Bristol, I had explored unsuccessfully some job opportunities that presented themselves. They came from the academy, in which I was much better known than I was within the ecclesiastical world. After the death of John Robinson, Trinity had to find a new Dean of Chapel and I asked the College (of which, because of my long service, I was a life Fellow, despite being away working as a curate) for my name to be considered. I was invited back for an interview, but I was not appointed. Looking back, I can now see how understandable it was for the College to choose an established and distinguished theologian from outside its ranks, rather than a beginner in that subject like myself, though naturally I had some pangs of disappointment at the time. More surprisingly, I was approached by an Oxford College and by a Cambridge College, both of which asked me if I would like to be considered as a possible Head. I went for interviews, and in one case was told informally that I had been put on a shortlist of two, but my illness intervened and in the end nothing came of either option.

As my curacy drew to a close, it began to be a rather pressing matter to try to find the next job. The authorities of the diocese of Bristol had made it clear from the start that they would not be in a position to offer me any future prospects. My mother had recently died peacefully of a final heart attack, after a week in the cottage hospital in Wells, visited by us and by her friends in the city, so that there was nothing to tie us any longer to living in the West of England. The diocese of Ely continued to take a friendly interest in me, but the only possibility available there was a rural parish with a strong Mattins/Book of Common Prayer tradition, which did not fit well with my Eucharist/modern liturgy preferences. For my own sake and for the sake of the parish, I felt that I had to decline this option. I then learned that there was a national clergy appointments adviser who maintained a file of priests seeking livings. I went to see him, my details were taken down and I was told that they would be circulated and that anyone interested would contact me direct.

In due course, some phone calls followed that were not particularly encouraging. I did not dispute that one must be prepared to go where God is calling one, but I doubted whether, for me, this was six small villages in the deepest Lincolnshire countryside. Eventually, one evening someone rang me up who explained that he was the vicar of two city-centre churches in Canterbury and also the Master of the Eastbridge Hospital, a medieval pilgrims' hospice now converted to a residential home for the elderly. This latter appointment made him Lord of the Manor of Blean, and consequently he was the patron of the living and responsible for finding a new vicar for that parish. 'Perhaps you don't know Blean?' he asked. I confessed ignorance, and I was told that it was a largish village two or three miles out of Canterbury. The University of Kent lay just outside the boundaries of the parish, giving obvious possibilities for contact with it and with its Anglican Chaplain. At last an interesting prospect seemed to have come into view.

The next step was to visit Blean, to look at it and to be looked at by the parish. I was met by the two churchwardens – Eric Bate, an agricultural scientist, and Fred Holmes, a 'fruitman', who had spent his working life employing his skills in the orchards that are so notable and beautiful a feature of that part of Kent. I took to both immediately, recognizing in them those qualities of good sense, faithfulness and reliability that any vicar would be grateful to have in those who were to be his friends and advisers. The village itself lies just off the main road from Canterbury to Whitstable. Topographically, it is a straggly sort of place, partly because, despite its being on the top of a rise, it is dotted with underground springs that hinder building on a number of sites. The church was medieval, with an attractive crown-post roof. It lies on the edge of the village, next to a site where there had once been a Roman villa. One could detect the occasional long thin Roman brick that had been incorporated into the church walls. The church's dedication is one that is rare in England, St Cosmas and St Damian, who were early Christian doctors and martyrs. In fact, due to the error of a medieval scribe in the relevant document, the literal dedication was one that must surely be unique in the whole of Christendom, for the first saint's name is spelt Cosmus, a local variation that has been carefully preserved down the centuries. The vicarage was modern, built on a plot carved out of the extensive grounds of a large Victorian vicarage now, thankfully, occupied (and heated) by a local solicitor. His wife kept a cow, Daisy, who would come and look at me when I worked in the vicarage garden.

I had a good day with the churchwardens and other parish representatives, and in due course I was offered, and accepted, the living. My proper title was Vicar in the Blean, for 'blean' is an Anglo-Saxon word whose root meaning is a piece of rough cloth, and so, by extension, a clearing in woodland, which is what Blean originally must have been. The village lies on the old Roman salt road from Canterbury to the port of Whitstable, and I liked to think, romantically but without any known historical justification, that we had been given our dedication by a Roman Christian who had remembered nostalgically the splendid church of Cosmas and Damian next to the Roman Forum.

When my appointment was announced, I was rung up in Bristol by a reporter who interviewed me for a piece that was to appear in the local paper. After the usual enquiries about wife and family and so on, he asked me if there was anything unusual about me that might interest his readers. I told him that I was a Fellow of the Royal Society. (In fact, at that time I was the only Church of England clergyman in the Royal, though I have since been joined by a colleague.) Any self-satisfaction I might have been feeling about my status was diminished when he innocently asked, 'Royal Society of what?'

My ecclesiastical superior as diocesan bishop was the Archbishop of

Canterbury, and Robert Runcie was kind enough one Saturday after-noon in 1984 to come along to take part in my induction and institution to the parish. The day-to-day running of the diocese was in the hands of one of his suffragans, the Bishop of Dover, who was, therefore, in the management-speak language that seems to be becoming more common today in the Church of England, my line manager.

Coming to a parish as its vicar is quite different from arriving as a curate. Assistant clergy come and go, but incumbents can have more serious and potentially long-term effects on a parish. They have, there-fore, to be scrutinized and evaluated more carefully by their parish-ioners. In the nature of things, there will be some people who simply regret that the new vicar is not the identical twin of the previous incum-bent, while for others this fact will be something to be held in favour of the new parson. These effects were not conspicuous at Blean when I arrived, though my predecessor Dick Maxwell and I were certainly very different kinds of people, and I could see that there were some parish-ioners who missed the old days. Soon after I had arrived, a much respected local doctor died, who had been an active member of the congregation, and it was obviously right that Dick should come back to take his funeral. After I had been at Blean about a year, I asked Dick to return again and to preach one Sunday, as well as leading the singing of a round at the end of the service, an act that had been a regular feature of his ministry but which was an accomplishment beyond the ability of his successor.

I inherited something from Dick Maxwell that I came to value greatly, and which I regard as having been one of the greatest of gifts he gave to our parish life. He had started a low-key but authentic healing ministry that took place once a month in the context of the Parish Eucharist, just before the exchange of the Peace. People were invited to come and kneel at the altar rails to seek healing by receiving the laying on of hands, administered alternately by the vicar and by a lay assistant who had been licensed for that purpose by the bishop. The two administrators had previously laid hands on each other, and the action in all cases was accompanied by the repetition of a simple prayer seeking the healing power of the Holy Spirit. People could come on their own behalf, or on behalf of another person. What was being sought remained the private knowledge alone of each person involved. In preparatory teaching it had been emphasized that healing is a search for wholeness, which may be given in many ways, ranging from physical recovery to the acceptance of what was happening, including possibly accepting the approach of death.

On any one Sunday on which this ministry was offered, at least a third of those present would come to the altar, the others being encouraged to pray silently as they remained in their pews. In the case of some of those who came forward, I might be able privately to guess why they did so, but in many other cases I had no idea what was being sought from God. The fact that one could come up for the healing of someone else helped to suppress any inappropriate curiosity about what a person's motives might have been. This healing ministry was a very real and powerful experience for all of us who took part in it. I am very glad that something very like it was started recently by the vicar in the parish in which I now live, and where it is clearly as much valued as it was in Blean.

A healing ministry of this kind was particularly appropriate in a church dedicated to St Cosmas and St Damian, for they are said to have treated their patients free and thus they can be reckoned to be patron saints of the National Health Service. There is a legend to the effect that they were pioneers of transplant surgery, for one sees paintings in which they have just grafted the leg of a black man onto a white patient's body! While at Blean, I learned from someone about some Russian Orthodox monks, living in a disused railway station near Walsingham, who paint modern icons in the traditional style. I wrote to ask them if they would paint me an icon of Cosmas and Damian. They did so and we used it in church on special festival occasions. People in the parish came to value the icon, and when we left Blean, Ruth and I had another one painted that we could leave behind as a farewell present to the parish.

Another important inherited parish custom at Blean was a monthly evening Requiem Eucharist, at which those who had died and whose anniversaries fell in that month would be remembered. The whole question of prayers for the dead has been a vexed one among the churches since Reformation times, but it seems to me only natural that Christians should find in Christ a unity in prayer with those they love, whether living or departed. (I pray for the departed close to me every day.) I was glad to continue this practice when I arrived in Blean, but I made one mistake in relation to the details. It had been customary to put a long list in the parish magazine of those who were due to be remembered that month. Without much thought, I suggested that this was not really necessary, and it was discontinued. No one protested to me at the time, but I noticed that as soon as I had left the parish, the practice was immediately restored. I had obviously failed to recognize that this was an important matter for a number of people.

Despite its being near the attractions of Canterbury, and despite its straggly topography, Blean was a very coherent village socially, and the church had a recognized role in what was going on in a self-contained community that was not always looking down the road to the city for its satisfactions. There was a good local primary school which was glad to have the vicar come in from time to time, but I have to confess that my talents and past experience had not made me God's gift to children, and that school activities of this kind, both in Kent and earlier in Bristol, were always ones that cost me a lot of effort and anxious preparation, however much I was grateful for the opportunity. Ruth was nursing part-time at Nunnery Fields, the local geriatric hospital, to which she travelled on a motor scooter, in order to avoid having to toil on a bicycle up the long stretch of St Thomas's Hill on her way home from tiring work.

We both found time to participate in village life. Ruth joined the Women's Institute and I the Gardeners' Club. (Gardening is the only practical activity at which I have any degree of competence. I planted a number of old-fashioned shrub roses in the vicarage garden, favourites of mine which there had the space to flourish as they should.) I used to go regularly to chat around at the afternoon meetings of the Pensioners' Club, where they always insisted in giving me not only a cup of tea but also a free raffle ticket, which seemed embarrassingly frequently to result in my winning a small prize, such as a packet of biscuits or a pot of jam.

I had been at Blean about a year when we discovered that some serious and costly work needed to be done on the chancel roof. We set about raising the money, and a gift day and some other activities quite soon brought in the sum we needed, with many contributions coming from villagers who valued the presence of their church, even if they did not often cross its threshold.

I could knock on any door in the village and expect to be asked in, and I used this privilege to be in touch with people whom I had heard were experiencing trouble of some kind, whether they came to church or not. There were funerals to take, weddings to perform and babies to baptize, again all activities involving a much wider range of people than those who were regular churchgoers. While I certainly believe in presenting the claims of Christ to Lordship over our lives, I believe that this is best done in a context of acceptance rather than judgement, a stance that not only fits my temperament but which, much more importantly, seems to be that which we find in the Gospels. People are often shy of expressing doubts or difficulties to a clergyman, and you need to listen carefully to try to discern what is really on their minds. They can feel that only the perfect would be acceptable to you. I remember talking to a devout woman who was about to marry a man whose first marriage had ended some time before they met, due to his first wife's desertion. She was enormously relieved when I asked her if she would like the marriage to be blessed in church, something that she had not felt able herself to ask for. There is a tendency for people to try to hide any doubt or perplexity from the clergy, a tactic that can create an atmosphere of unreality in conversation. I am not myself the sort of person who has been given the gift of a totally untroubled faith. Sometimes Christianity seems to me to be just too good to be true, but when that sort of doubt arises I say to myself, 'All right then, deny it,' and I know that is something I could never do. I have to stand on Christ's side.

The general English attitude to religion is an oblique one. On average, people are not great church attenders, but surveys consistently show a significant majority who either call themselves Christian or say that they believe in God. A kind of folk religion is very widespread, sometimes rather superstitious and often centred on a notion that there is Someone Up There who has an eye on you and who just might, if you behave yourself, let you win the National Lottery one week. When I visited people, they would quite often tell me that they said their prayers, though it did not seem to occur to many of them to try doing so occasionally with others in church. Of course, to some extent politeness drives people to say to you what they think will please you, but I believe the claim being made was quite often true, even if the prayers might have been simply of a 'Please give me . . .' kind. I do not despise folk religion, though I am saddened by its shallowness and its misapprehensions about the nature of God. What any priest must long for, and is sometimes given the chance to be able to do, is to lead people to know the God and Father of our Lord Jesus Christ.

Part of the deal in my going to Blean had been that I would have a little time to devote to academic work, particularly to the task of thinking and writing about science and religion which, oddly enough, I had only recently come to recognize clearly as being a part of my vocation. I had been thinking on and off about these matters as I wandered round the streets of Windmill Hill, but I had had no time then to attempt coherent writing. Now at Blean, it became possible to put something on paper. I shall discuss my theological writings in a later chapter, but let me now just note that I wrote *One World* while in Kent, dedicating it to my friends, the Sisters at Tymawr. I also had some contact with the University of Kent, which kindly made me an honorary professor of physics. An important consequence of the latter appointment was that I acquired a parking badge which I could use when visiting the University Library.

Ruth and I made many good friends in Blean, with some of whom we remained in regular contact. It was a very happy time for us there. After I had been Vicar for about two years, I went to have a chat with my ecclesiastical boss, the Bishop of Dover. I said how much I was enjoying my ministry and how we both enjoyed village life. I recognized, however, that the academic and intellectual side of me was not being greatly exercised. I tried Sunday by Sunday to preach in a responsible and truthful manner, and I was always glad to talk to anyone who showed an interest in how science and religion relate to each other, but I did not think it necessary or right to force this latter issue, so personally absorbing to me, on others for whom it was not particularly significant. I therefore told the bishop that I hoped that sometime I might find a position that combined a pastoral care with an active intellectual task of some suitable kind. He said he understood what I was saying, and I felt sure that he did. I thought that I was simply putting up a marker for what I might hope to be able to do in a few years' time. In view of the Church's somewhat relaxed attitude to career development, it seemed wise to use any opportunity that came one's way to make clear any simple aspiration one had, without expecting immediate fulfilment. I was certainly not asking for, or contemplating, an immediate move.

Just a very few months later my phone rang, and someone I knew at Trinity Hall (a more ancient College than Trinity and situated next door to it in Cambridge) told me that that College was looking for a new Dean of Chapel and it would like to consider me for the post. I made it clear that I was very interested, but also that I would need to think carefully before making a move again so soon. Anyway, I duly went for an interview, and I was offered the job. I had only been a vicar for just over two years; we were both happy in Blean – Ruth perhaps particularly so, as she really enjoyed village life – and I felt troubled at the idea of leaving the parish after so short a time. The next step was to talk it all over with the Bishop of Dover. After I had explained both the opportunity presented and my hesitations about taking it, he said to me that he felt I had been offered the job that I had described to him at our last conversation together, and that I should very seriously consider taking it. This was helpful and generous advice. After further reflection, I decided to accept a post that would combine conducting the worship of Chapel and having a pastoral care in the College community, with being Director of Studies in theology and having time, particularly in vacation, to pursue my own intellectual interests. Ruth loyally acquiesced in the decision, though she was reluctant to leave Blean.

The people of St Cosmus and St Damian were generous in accepting this decision and they gave me and Ruth a heartwarming send-off. Thus it came about that, having left Cambridge in 1982 with an expectation that my future working life was to be in the parochial ministry, I found myself in the somewhat embarrassing position of returning to the academic fold after only a little more than four years away. University people who live in Cambridge tend to think that there is really nowhere else to be. On our return, friends would come up to us and say, 'You must be very glad to be back.' I tried to explain that it was a bit more complicated than that. Ruth sometimes just said no, though she good-naturedly soon settled in to being again in the city where we had already spent so much of our married life.

13

Trinity Hall

When we returned to Cambridge, Ruth continued geriatric nursing, but now as an agency nurse, since College life involved us both in social engagements that meant that she had to be able to specify some time in advance the days on which she was available for work. We also had to become active yet again in the housing market. While we had been in Blean, we had sold our house in Belvoir Road and bought a nicely refurbished flat in Bateman Street. The idea had been that Michael would live there while he was training to become an accountant and that all of us could use it as a convenient pied-à-terre when visiting the city. These plans were now frustrated by our return. Michael had to be told the sad news that rent-free accommodation would no longer be on offer, since Ruth and I needed to live in the flat for some months while we looked round for a larger property that would be suitable for the longer term. After some searching, we moved into a house in north Cambridge, in Hurst Park Avenue, which is still my home. It is a between-the-wars house, sufficiently far out to have a garage and a driveway so that one does not have the problem of parking in the road, yet it is also within easy cycling distance of the centre. When living nearer into the city, as we did when we were in Belvoir Road, we had often felt somewhat reluctant to drive off in case there was no parking space available in the road on one's return. It was good to get settled satisfactorily in our new home, and a relief to know that the period in which we seemed regularly to have been paying Cambridge estate agents' fees had come to an end.

Quite soon after our return, our first grandchild, Katherine, was born. The day after her birth, we learned that she had been diagnosed as having Down's syndrome. We had been anxious to see her as soon as possible in any case, but now it became very important to do so straight away, in order that we got to know her from the first as a person and so to avoid any temptation to think of her as a 'problem'. The next day we drove down to visit Katherine and Isobel in hospital. Like all our grand-children, Katherine has been a great joy to us. With the loving care of her parents, and with some skilled help in the course of her education, she has grown into a much-loved and happy young woman.

I began to settle into the job of being a College Dean. Trinity Hall was quite different from its younger and much larger trinitarian neighbour that I knew so well. Becoming its Dean also meant that I became a Fellow of the Hall. This fact, agreeable though it was in itself in so many ways, also had a somewhat sad consequential side effect, for it automatically terminated my life Fellowship at Trinity. Of course, it was entirely reasonable that one should not simultaneously be a Fellow of two Colleges, but the ending of a formal link with the institution where I had been a student, and then a Fellow for more than 30 years, was a kind of bereavement for me. Gut feelings do not change too readily. I would certainly henceforth cheer on Trinity Hall boats taking part in the bumping races on the river, but there would be a secret internal satisfaction if First and Third Trinity were also doing well.

Trinity is the largest and richest college at either Cambridge or Oxford. Trinity Hall is one of the smallest Cambridge Colleges. It seemed in my time there to be reasonably comfortably off, but without signs of exceptional riches. I enjoyed the domestic scale and intimate atmosphere of the Hall, and the fact that it was a College that took food seriously, with good consequences for the meals at High Table. The High Table Steward was Roy Calne, whose international fame as a transplant surgeon took him to many countries from which he would bring back recipes and materials that would then appear on our menus. Colleges are idiosyncratic institutions, each with its own particular style, so that what would be inconceivable at one may turn out to be a daily practice at another. One of the greatest shocks I received on joining the Hall was to find that custom permitted Fellows, if they wished, to read newspapers while lunching at the common board in the Senior Combination Room. (The latter is a uniquely Cantabridgian word for what elsewhere would be called a Common Room.) I instantly took a private vow that I would never avail myself of this dubious privilege, which I considered an unjustifiable threat to general conversation. Throughout my time at Trinity Hall I remained faithful to this commitment and, in fairness, I have to admit that most other Fellows were, in fact, similarly abstemious. One of the best customs at the Hall was that the High Table dinner on Tuesdays was for Fellows only, with no guests allowed. The great majority of Fellows then in residence (there would always be some away on sabbatical leave) would come in to dine that evening. The resulting conviviality did much to maintain unity and a good spirit in the Fellowship.

The College Chapel was small – in fact, the smallest of the ancient College Chapels in Cambridge – and it had been involved in the classical face-lift that the Hall had given its ancient buildings when fashions changed in the eighteenth century. The first impression was of a classical building, but if you went behind Chapel you could see the original roughness of the medieval walls, which in front had been covered over with smooth ashlar. The Chapel's intimate space was helpful to worship. On Sunday, we had College Communion in the morning, followed by the inducement to worship given by the cooked breakfast provided by the kitchens specially for Chapel attenders. Sunday evening there was Evensong conducted according to the Book of Common Prayer (the most successful BCP service, I believe, as far as modern use is concerned), with some good music provided by the organ scholars and a volunteer undergraduate choir. I said the Office in Chapel on weekdays, except Saturdays, usually joined in the morning by Jonathan Steinberg, an urbane and intellectually stimulating history don who was to prove a good friend to me. Occasionally an undergraduate might drop in to one of these short weekday services, and once a week there was

Choral Evensong with the choir. I could have organized a rota that ensured that each day there was an undergraduate lesson reader in Chapel, but I decided not to do so as I was reluctant to impose attendance as an occasional duty to be demanded of the faithful. Looking back on it now, I am not sure this was the right decision, as I think that the experience of attendance at the Office might have been good for some people.

Being a College Dean was very different from being a vicar. Most of my flock were aged 18 to 22 and most would only be there for three years. The community and congregation that one served was in a state of regular flux. Moreover, its members were only there for about half the year. When any great festival, such as Christmas or Easter, was on the horizon, they all disappeared. Undergraduates are mostly charming people, but also mostly unreliable to some degree, with many competing distractions in their lives. They tend to come when they feel like it. I had a sequence of dependable undergraduate Chapel Clerks, but often I sighed for a pair of totally reliable churchwardens, the kind of people whom you knew would be there, come what may, even if they had to trudge through flood or snow to get to church.

My official position was Dean and Chaplain, the former carrying responsibility for Chapel worship and an expectation of academic activity, the latter implying a duty of pastoral care in the College community. I tried to be available pastorally to students, but this was not an easy task for me to discharge. At my age, the College bar late at night was not my natural habitat, and it would have been false to pretend the contrary. Yet that might well have been a fruitful field to cultivate, had I been able to do so naturally. In a parish, I had relied on visiting for a good many of my pastoral contacts. The conventions of College life included the privacy of one's own room, a privilege rightly valued by undergraduates, but one that did not make it appropriate for me just to go round knocking on doors without some prior indication that this would be acceptable. I did some entertaining in my own rooms but, I think now, not as much as I might have done. The pastoral care of the College staff was an easier matter, more akin to parochial work. If I heard that one of the

The Society of Ordained Scientists, of which I was one of the founders, along with Arthur Peacocke, Warden (pictured front, left) and John Habgood, Visitor (front, centre)

porters or one of the cooks was ill, I could visit their homes and seek to be of some help. Similarly, I could visit a Fellow who was in hospital (or an undergraduate for that matter, though that did not happen very often) and I also had a number of interesting and serious conversations with colleagues, believing or unbelieving, about the Christian faith. On the whole, I was clearly more effective in the role of Dean than in the role of Chaplain.

The Master of Trinity Hall, Sir John Lyons, a distinguished linguistics scholar, was a Roman Catholic and a supporter of Sunday evening Chapel. One day, I got a letter from the senior Roman Catholic Chaplain in the University, based at Fisher House, calling my attention to the fact that the pope was just about to beatify 40 English martyrs executed in the reign of Queen Elizabeth I. One of these was a Trinity Hall man, and the Chaplain suggested that we might like to mark this notable event by having a Roman Catholic Mass in Chapel. I thought so too, and I knew how much this would please the Master. Accordingly plans went ahead and one evening the Roman Catholic priest arrived with his equipe (thurifers, acolytes) for what I believe was the first such Mass in Trinity Hall Chapel since the Reformation. The building was packed for what was a great occasion, with a good number of unusual faces in the congregation. One could easily tell who was who, for when the priest said, 'Let us pray', all the Roman Catholics stood up and all the Anglicans and others knelt down. As a generous gesture, I had been invited to preach. I took the opportunity to express my hopes for ecumenism and my longing for Christian unity, as well as sorrow and repentance for the grievous mistakes of the past in the way in which Christians had treated each other. It seemed right to remind the congregation that there was another Trinity Hall martyr whom we should also remember, Thomas Bilney, burnt at the stake in 1531 for his Protestant convictions.

The oddest incident that took place in Chapel during my time occurred at a Sunday Evensong. The New Testament lesson set for the day was John 8.1–11, the story of the woman taken in adultery. This is a floating piece of tradition that in some ancient manuscripts appears at other places in John, and even occasionally in Luke. (Nevertheless, I believe it to be a genuine reminiscence of Jesus.) As a consequence of this variable tradition, the modern version of the Bible that we had on the Chapel lectern had cautiously placed the story at the end of John, as a kind of appendix. The undergraduate who came up to read the lesson found himself in the nightmare situation of having to read the first 11 verses of a chapter which, in the text in front of him, began at verse 12! For a moment he stood speechless, but I guessed immediately what the situation was and I was able to rush forward to find the right place for him.

As far as the academic side of my responsibilities was concerned, I had a small number of students reading theology in the Hall, whom I had helped to choose and whose studies I then directed when they came up into residence. I also gave a course of lectures in the University for the Theological and Religious Studies Tripos, providing an introduction to science and theology issues, and I set and marked the exam paper relating to this course. I supervised undergraduates taking this course, whether they were at Trinity Hall or not, and I arranged for my own students to be supervised by dons in other Colleges in topics I was not competent to deal with myself. There was a good deal of friendly taking in each other's washing of this kind in the Faculty of Divinity. I had time to write two books on science and religion, one of which, *Science and Providence*, I dedicated to the Master, Fellows and Scholars of Trinity Hall. I also did some teaching on science and religion for the Federation of Cambridge Theological Seminaries. There was an interesting difference in ethos between this work and university teaching. In the latter case, a somewhat detached academic stance was appropriate, but with an audience of ordinands one could presume a shared Christian faith.

Cambridge Colleges are self-governing institutions and the Fellows act as the Trustees. Legally the separate Colleges are independent of each other and of the University itself, but realistically they have common interests that encourage close collaboration between all parties. Some tasks are reserved to the University (such as formal lectures and laboratory work, and the awarding of degrees), while others are the province of individual Colleges (selecting students, supervisions, board and lodging). Constitutionally, the situation bears some analogy to the relationship between the Federal Government and the states in the USA.

In Trinity, a College that even in my time already had more than a hundred Fellows, all but the most significant decisions, such as putting up a new building, were delegated to the College Council, elected by the Fellows from among themselves. Trinity Hall, however, was small enough for this stratagem not to be necessary, and the whole Fellowship regularly met as the Governing Body to discuss and (usually) ratify decisions proposed to it by its various Committees. The charm of College life lies largely in the fact that these academic communities are really intimate entities, and their scale is such that they act socially as villages within the greater conurbation of the University. They are places where all have something particular to contribute and where all can feel that they are playing a significant role in the society.

I was very content at Trinity Hall and I would have been happy to work there till retirement. However, one day my phone rang and someone whom I knew a little from my DAMTP days, said, 'You may know that we are looking for a new President at Queens'. Would you like to be considered?' President is the title Queens' College gives to its Head. I had been in this situation of being canvassed for Head of a House before, but now I was much more settled than I could have been in my curate days, the time when I had previously been under consideration for such an academic position. I was doing a job that made use both of my priestly vocation and of my academic experience and interests. Consequently, I was not anxious for a move, but my enquirer required some sort of instant response. I said that I would be glad to be considered, but if things got really serious I would need to think more carefully about what I ought to do if I did receive the invitation. My caller said that he understood that, and he supposed that doubtless I, in turn, understood that matters were at a preliminary investigative stage in Queens' and nothing might come of it, in which case I would not have to worry about making a decision. I agreed. On that note, our conversation ended.

Eventually it turned out that I was to leave Trinity Hall, and I was greatly touched and honoured that after my departure the College made me an Honorary Fellow.

14

Queens' College

<hr>

Following the telephone call from Queens', nothing happened for about two or three weeks. I then received a message from the Vice-President inviting me to come to dinner one evening and meet with the Fellows afterwards 'to answer a few questions'. I went along, behaved nicely at the High Table and then settled down to what proved to be an hour and a half's conversation with a large group of the Fellowship. I was not at all sure in my own mind whether being President would be the right move for me and so I felt fairly relaxed. It was a purely secular job for which I was being considered, but the fact that there was a Chapel in Queens', whose Dean, the philosophical theologian Brian Hebblethwaite, was known to me, and that I could expect to play a role in the College's worshipping life, made the position conceivable in a way that a purely university job of some kind would not have been. I decided that I would just enjoy the evening's conversation, say frankly whatever was in my mind, and simply see what happened. Towards the end of what had proved to be a stimulating encounter, Brian Hebblethwaite asked me whether we had any pets. I detected an increased attentiveness in the room at this point and it occurred to me that this might well turn out to be a critical question. I said that we did not and I had the distinct impression of a feeling of relief in my audience at this reply. I learned later that the recent incumbents of the President's Lodge had had a small and somewhat snappy dog, not universally beloved in Queens'. A pet-less

President was high on the Queens' agenda. At the end of the evening, I was thanked for having come and I was escorted out of the College.

Again two or three weeks went by, and then another phone call invited me to bring my wife in to lunch so that afterwards we could meet a smaller group of Fellows for further talk. Clearly matters were getting serious. I decided I must seek some advice to help me in thinking what I should do if I were actually to be offered the job. I contacted three senior bishops who knew me and, interestingly and helpfully, they all essentially gave me the same independent advice. Each said he believed that there was value to the Christian community at large if some ordained priests occupied positions of significant secular responsibility, provided they had the past experience that qualified them for such a role. I saw the point that was being made, though I can now admit that I would have preferred to have been able to undertake a greater responsibility within the community of the Church, rather than alongside it in the academy. However, it seemed pretty clear that that was not going to be an option for me.

Eventually I was invited to become the new President of Queens'. (I gathered later that the final decision had lain between me and a distinguished internal candidate, and I would like to acknowledge that the latter treated me with kindness and generous acceptance when I arrived in the College.) There was, however, a matter that had to be cleared up before I felt able to accept the offer. Like many other Colleges, Queens' had some 'double sets', rooms occupied by two undergraduates sharing. The rule had been that the pairs involved should be of the same sex, but there was now pressure from the undergraduate body to have this changed. When I received the College's invitation, this issue was still under consideration by the Governing Body. My own moral belief is the traditional Christian understanding that sexual intimacy is properly to be expressed within the faithful bond of marriage, but I understood, of course, that all do not accept this and I understood also that, with the change in the age of legal majority, Colleges no longer stood *in loco parentis* in relation to their junior members, so that it would be inappropriate for the authorities to attempt to act as general moral censors of

Queens', Cambridge, with the President's Lodge above

private behaviour, even if they had wished to do so. However, it seemed to me that allowing mixed sharing would be to give public and institutional endorsement of a moral position with which I would not feel it right to be associated. I explained to the Fellowship that I would not be able to accept the Presidency if mixed sharing became College policy in Queens'. I waited, therefore, to see what the Governing Body would decide. In the end the change was not agreed, and I became Queens' fortieth President since its foundation in 1448.

Ruth and I moved into the President's Lodge in September 1989. It was a truly splendid home to live in, even if one knew that it was for a limited period only. (Later one of our grandchildren was to express real disappointment when he learned that this was not our permanent home.) The oldest part of the Lodge had been built as part of Old Court, the foundational College buildings completed about 1450 and the first collegiate structures in Cambridge to be made of brick. Today, Old Court is the best preserved fifteenth-century court at either Oxford or Cambridge, a medieval college in miniature. A range of rooms next to the river was added to the President's accommodation in the later fifteenth century. This part of the Lodge included a handsome panelled dining room, the Audit Room, which had served in earlier times as a guest room and audience chamber for distinguished visitors to the College. I liked to tell those dining with us that Catherine of Aragon had slept where we were then eating. If the Fellows of Queens' had had the money, all this magnificence would have been swept away in the classicizing frenzy of the eighteenth century. In architectural matters, comparative poverty can sometimes prove to be a blessing.

These two fifteenth-century halves of the Lodge were joined together in the following century by a half-timbered Elizabethan Long Gallery that is one of the famous rooms of Cambridge. We do not know precisely when it was built, since no record of this, or any receipt for payment, survives in the College archives. The everyday use of this splendid Gallery was as a corridor linking my studies (I had two, a formal one for meetings and a working garret for writing) to the living quarters of the Lodge, but it also made an admirable setting for drinks receptions. Once a year, the St Margaret's Society, the College music club, gave a chamber concert in the Long Gallery. We all enjoyed this elegant occasion, but it also gave me some anxiety, for it required a party of undergraduates to manhandle a harpsichord up a rather handsome staircase into the Gallery. There was never an accident, but there were moments when it seemed a frightful possibility.

Not only was the Lodge beautiful and historic, but it was also very liveable in. The rooms were of a size that succeeded in combining grandeur with domesticity. Ruth and I could sit on our own of an evening in our drawing room without feeling that we were in some sort of museum piece, but the same room could readily accommodate ten guests drinking coffee with us after dinner.

Shortly after we had moved in, there was a national census which also included a questionnaire about the accommodation that people were occupying. One query asked how many rooms you had, not counting kitchen and bathrooms. Our answer was 20. And how many people live on the premises? Our reply was two. We resisted the urge to write in the margin that this was not as scandalous an over-provision as it might seem. In fact, in one way or another, we made use of all the rooms at our disposal. Of course, we needed the help of staff in running such a big home. Here we were very fortunate. Our housekeeper, Glenys Nixon, was a skilled and inventive cook, whose style was different from that of the College kitchens, a fact much appreciated by Fellows who were, of course, very familiar with the repertoire of the latter. The job of keeping everything spick and span was efficiently performed by two ladies, Janette Carter and Dawn Scott, whose work included polishing daily the brass plaque on the front door that said 'President'. Soon after my arrival, I needed to appoint a new personal secretary. Jo Brown provided me with the willing support and total dependability that were of great importance to me, both in the discharge of my College duties and also for my academic work in science and theology. Together, we formed a happy small community centred on the Lodge, and Ruth and I were very grateful for all that our staff gave us during our time in Queens'.

While we lived in College, we rented out our house in Hurst Park Avenue to a succession of visiting scholars and their families. We met some interesting people in this way and they proved to be considerate tenants. No doubt this was not only because there is a natural fellow feeling among academics, but also because they too would have rented out their own homes while away and so, in their turn, they were sensitive to issues of caring for someone else's property.

Arriving in a College as the Head of the House requires the ascent of a steep learning curve. New conventions have to be accepted and a new set of ancestors acquired. One of my essential preliminary tasks was a careful reading of the College history. I had to learn something of my predecessors, who included John Fisher, beheaded by Henry VIII and later canonized by the pope, and Isaac Milner, mathematician and university politician, active at the turn of the eighteenth century, a big man in every sense of the word, whose personal chair in the Long Gallery had the appearance of a small settee. The most famous person who had ever spent time in Queens' was Desiderius Erasmus, brought to Cambridge by Fisher to teach Greek and the New Learning. He completed his scholarly edition of the Greek New Testament while in the College and we still have in our Library the copy that he gave to Queens'. Erasmus' longest stay was about two and a half years, after which he returned to continental Europe, having complained that in Cambridge the east wind is cold (it still is) and the beer thin (now improved). However, he did admit to liking what was then the English custom of greeting ladies by kissing them on both cheeks. Erasmus was a great man, but one has to recognize that he was also a bit of a whinger.

When you arrive in a new College, colleagues will offer you advice, some of which will be good, but not all of it, and you have to try to work out quickly which is which. The most important thing to realize about being Head of a Cambridge College is that you are not the Chief Executive. The democratic character of the donnish community means that the President does not have a great deal of directly exercisable power of personal decision. He has to work with the other College 'Officers of State' (the Senior Tutor in charge of the educational side; the Senior Bursar in charge of finances; the Junior Bursar in charge of the buildings and domestic arrangements), as well as with the Governing Body (in Queens', all the Fellows with long-term appointments), which will have the final say on any major decision. The President presides over the Governing Body as well as preparing its Agenda, and also takes the chair at all principal College committees. This gives the President a good deal of influence and offers many opportunities for guiding College policy. I am not temperamentally a CEO, so that having to work by seeking to establish consensus suited me well. If one is acting as chairman of a committee, I think it is essential that one approaches the meeting with a possible set of outcomes in mind for how the business might work out, but one needs also sufficient flexibility of attitude to be able to recognize when opinion is flowing in a direction different from that which you had anticipated. It is your responsibility to facilitate finding a mutually acceptable way ahead. I did not invariably manage to get agreement to what I believed would have been the best decision to make, but I never felt that the College had taken a decision so unwise that I ought to consider my own position. My image of being President was that of a constitutional monarch – but of an eighteenth-century rather than contemporary kind, so that there was more to it than simply a symbolic or decorative dimension.

A more modest image than the monarchical, and one that reflected a somewhat different side of being President, was that of the village squire. In the College community of dons, students and staff, the President had the standing of being first among equals, together with the social responsibilities attaching to such a status. One aspect of this squirearchical dimension was that we did a lot of entertaining. There were particular occasions and special visits (the most notable of which was our Patroness, Queen Elizabeth the Queen Mother, coming to open Lyon Court, named in her honour), but there was also a programme of steady hospitality. Ruth and I liked a regular life and so we entertained in a regular way. On Saturdays, freshers came to breakfast in batches of a dozen at a time. This excellent idea had been taken over from our predecessors, Ron and Ursula Oxburgh. Breakfast is an informal meal (people could come dressed more or less as they liked) and it has a natural end, for in Cambridge there are nine o'clock lectures even on Saturdays. (Freshers often find it difficult to know when to leave – I told our children when they went to university that if they wanted to earn the undying gratitude of the dons they should be prepared to make the first move to leave a party.) The relatively small company allowed some general conversation and I was always keen to ensure that everyone was drawn into this. I had been a shyish undergraduate myself and I knew that some people would need encouragement. Before our guests left, I took them on a short tour of the Long Gallery, telling them a bit about the history of the College in the process. We had in the Gallery a late-fifteenth-century chair that was called the chair of Erasmus – after all, he might have sat on it and we needed a relic of the great man. I used to tell the students how eventually Erasmus had returned 'to Europe'. One day, as he was saying goodbye, a very nice German undergraduate said to me most courteously, 'When you said Europe, I expect you meant the continent.' I blushed, acknowledging my need to speak more carefully in future.

Third-year students came to lunch on Sundays, a meal that took the traditional British form of roast meat and two veg, followed by a fruit pie or crumble. By this time of their university careers, these young men and women had no need of any encouragement to talk. They were socially adroit, put you at your ease, and kept the conversation going. It was pleasant to see this enhanced maturity, no doubt a lot of it due simply to being three years older, but some of it deriving from their Cambridge education. The 'treat' for the third years was being taken after lunch into my formal study to look through a spy-hole which had enabled the President in those centuries when he kept himself more to himself than is the case today, to cast an eye on what the Fellows might be up to, dining at the High Table in the Old Hall below.

Every Wednesday evening we had a dinner party for colleagues in Queens' and friends and visitors from outside. Glenys provided her excellent food and we borrowed the College butler for the evening in order to supervise its serving. It was an agreeable and trouble-free way of entertaining. At the end of the evening, Ruth would take the coffee cups downstairs to be washed up by Janette and Dawn in the morning, while I put away any silver still left out, and then we went to bed.

There were also drinks parties in the Long Gallery for graduate students, and for senior College staff, and an annual pensioners' tea party in our walled garden. A particular pleasure for us in vacation time was to be able to have all our family to stay for Christmas or New Year in a College that, lacking staff and students at that time of the year, was unnaturally quiet for a few days. There was only one real snag to living in the Lodge. In the summer tourist season there was a lot of noise from the river. In Ruth's and my undergraduate days, punting had been an elegant relaxation for those who knew what they were doing. It had now become a kind of tourist funfair, as visitors, unable instantly to master the subtle art required, collided with each other or with the banks, all the while shouting with laughter. I never actually poured a bucket of water over some noisy party, but at times the temptation was strong. However, things quietened down in the evening, as the tour buses returned to London. An occasional late evening pleasure was to hear a solitary canoeist who used to play elegiac airs on his flute as he drifted down-stream.

Heads of Houses sometimes entertain on behalf of the Vice-Chancellor, particularly by looking after persons about to receive honorary degrees whose intellectual interests have some connection with that of their host. One year, we had as a guest Paul Erdos, a brilliant and eccentric Hungarian mathematician who never had a home of his own but roamed the world with his suitcase, stopping off where he thought interesting mathematics might be going on. He had asked to have breakfast in bed on the morning of the degree ceremony and this was duly provided. We had to be at the Senate House by ten to meet the Chancellor, the Duke of Edinburgh. When Erdos had not come down by 9.30, I thought I had better go up to see what was happening. To my relief, I found him nearly fully dressed. 'Do you think I ought to wear a tie?' he asked me. 'I have one, but I do not know how to tie it. You must do it for me.' I said that I thought that a tie would be a desirable accessory on this formal occasion. However, I could not manage the mirror-reversed movements that were required if I were to tie it on him, so I had to tie it on myself and then loosen the knot for transfer to Professor Erdos. Fortunately the rest of the morning then went without a hitch.

An annual event to which I always looked forward was the graduation ceremony at the end of June. In Oxford, graduations are sporadic events taking place throughout the year, but at Cambridge we have the better idea of concentrating matters so that most people are able to graduate in the company of their College contemporaries. The days of General Admission are taken up with successive cohorts of graduands coming from the different Colleges to receive their degrees in the Senate House. The actual degree is conveyed individually by means of the Vice-Chancellor or a Deputy uttering the appropriate Latin formula as the candidate kneels in an act of homage to learning. The order in which these collegiate cohorts come is largely determined by the date of foundation of their College, and this meant that Queens' and St Catherine's College made up two halves of one of the sessions. Turn and turn about, every other year either I or the Master of St Catherine's had the privilege of being the VC's Deputy for this session, a task that I greatly enjoyed in the years in which it fell to me. Afterwards we had a grand lunch in Queens' for the new graduates and their parents. It was a happy event – as I recall it now, the sun always shone – and it gave me a chance in my speech to express the College's thanks to the assembled parents for the support they had given their children in their university careers. Unless there had been some particular problems, it was only on this final occasion that I really got to meet many of the parents.

A more routine aspect of College life for us was that Ruth and I worshipped regularly in the College Chapel in term time. Brian Hebblethwaite retired from being Dean in the middle of my period of office, and he was succeeded by Jonathan Holmes, a veterinary scientist who had been acting as Chaplain for a number of years previously. I celebrated Holy Communion regularly in Chapel and preached once a term at Sunday Evensong, as well as at Communion services. This active association with the Christian community in Queens' was very important to me and it confirmed the conviction that I had been right to accept being President.

Queens' was different in character from my two previous Colleges. Numerically it lay on the larger side of the Cambridge average, admitting about 150 undergraduates each year. The accidents of history have not been all that kind to Queens' in the matter of financial resources. The College's first Foundress was Margaret of Anjou, the wife of the saintly but ineffectual Henry VI. He had founded King's College, but his strongminded wife had ambitions for a College of her own. A Cambridge rector, Andrew Doket, who had been trying unsuccessfully to found a College of St Bernard, got wind of this. He proposed to Queen Margaret that she should found a College dedicated to St Margaret of Antioch and St Bernard of Clairvaux. The idea appealed to the Queen and the new foundation was set up right next door to Henry's King's College. Doket became the first President. (There does not seem to have been any significance in choosing this title in preference to the more usual Cambridge usage of 'Master'. In fact, in Queens' the vocative of President is Master, and I was so addressed on formal occasions, such as Governing Body meetings.) In 1461, Henry was deposed and Edward IV took the throne. Doket judged that this was the time to change sides in the Wars of the Roses, making a switch from the Lancastrians to the Yorkists. In 1465, Edward's Queen, Elizabeth Woodville, became our second Foundress, a fact that explains the position of the apostrophe in the College's name. When Richard III succeeded Edward, his wife, Anne Neville, also took an interest in Queens' and persuaded Richard to make a substantial bene-faction to the College. Unfortunately, however, he then lost the Battle of Bosworth and, in the sad words of the recital at the Commemoration of Benefactors which I read every year, Henry VII 'resumed' what Richard had given. As a result, Queens' has always had to be somewhat careful about what it can afford. Even today, we have not wholly recovered from the consequences of the Battle of Bosworth.

I enjoyed and respected the ethos of Queens'. It seemed to me that the College took academic pursuits seriously, but without stifling a lively social and sporting side to its activities. The College had some very successful years in the Tripos, reaping the fruit of a well-thought-out recruitment policy initiated earlier by a Senior Tutor, John Green, and an Admissions Tutor, Andrew Phillips, who together set out to encourage bright applicants from schools which did not often send pupils to Oxbridge.

The historian and philosopher of science Thomas Kuhn liked to speak of periods of 'normal science', concerned with problem-solving within an existing conceptual framework, and periods of 'revolutionary science' in which that framework itself was undergoing radical revision. Kuhn overdid the contrasts somewhat, but there is a degree of truth in this kind of alternating pattern of change and consolidation. Similarly, academic institutions have their contrasting periods, times of normal growth and development, and times of more significant change (new buildings, new administrative or educational arrangements, and so on). My Presidency fell into the normal, consolidatory mode. I endeavoured to get to know as many Old Members as I could, a task in which I had, of course, to start practically from scratch. In my time, we received some

*I have been lucky enough to meet a number of interesting and well-known people.
This meeting was in the Vatican*

generous benefactions, but I had told the Fellows when they interviewed me that, though I would do my best, I was not a naturally gifted fund-raiser. In any case, a major effort in that respect was scheduled for 1998, when the College would celebrate its 550th anniversary. By then I had retired (1996) and been succeeded by John Eatwell, an economist and also a member of the House of Lords. He has been a vigorous and enterprising Head of the House and I have the happiness of having every confidence in my successor.

15

Theological Writing

———⊰•⊱———

I love writing. It is one of my favourite occupations. Partly this is due to the challenge presented by the need to use words as clearly and effectively as possible. If I feel that I have succeeded in explaining something in an accessible and well-organized way, then the pedagogic side of me is really pleased. Another great satisfaction given by writing is the fact that the author is in charge. No one else tells you what you have to write. In many other activities, one has to adjust to the views of colleagues, trying to find consensus through being prepared to compromise a little. In writing, the decisions and judgements are entirely one's own. But perhaps the greatest satisfaction of all that comes from writing is finding out what you actually think. One reads the thoughts of others, and, as one reflects on that reading, ideas buzz around in one's own mind. Maybe this; maybe that. When the moment comes to put something down on paper, you have to decide what it is that you actually believe and want to say. The act of writing is the act of the crystallization of thought. John Robinson once said to me that he could not really think without a pen in his hand. I knew immediately what he meant.

I do any serious writing using a ball-point pen and A4 paper. Later the draft will be committed to a word processor, but I cannot type fast enough to keep up with myself when the thought is flowing, so initial composition has to be in long-hand. In the days when I had a secretary, Jo would marvellously decipher my almost illegible scribble and transfer it onto the computer. Now I have to do that task for myself, just as in the very earliest days of authorship I had typed things out on a rattly portable typewriter. I do not begrudge the time spent in this activity, for it gives you a close acquaintance with the text, and a certain number of errors and infelicities come to light in the process. I do not naturally write with very good syntax and there is always work of improvement to be done in this respect, though some errors will remain undetected until the eagle eye of a copy-editor spots them. For many people, and certainly for myself, the key to being able to write reasonably well is being able to spot when you have written unreasonably badly, so that you can then try to put it right. I am a revisionary writer and I welcome the ease in making changes afforded by the use of a computer. In particular I like, if at all possible, to put aside a manuscript for a couple of months or so, in order to reread and revise it after a fallow period. In the first flush of composition, one can often feel rather pleased with a chapter which, on later reflection, turns out not to be quite as wonderful as one had first thought.

The decision that my vocation should include a fair amount of activity in the area of science and religion has involved me in a good deal of speaking around, as well as in writing. I enjoy interacting with an audience, and for me the best part of such an occasion is the discussion period at the end. After all, I know what I am going to say, but I don't know what they are going to say. You have to set some sort of provisional agenda for the conversation by giving a set-piece talk first, but then the audience can choose its own agenda, and in responding to that you know that you are addressing issues that really matter to those present. (It is striking how often questions about suffering surface, whatever the formal subject of the talk may have been.) I like as much as possible to speak from notes and not from a full text. I think that I am more interesting to listen to in that more discursive mode, though the 'spontaneous' words spoken inevitably often contain a degree of self-quotation from earlier writings, as happy phrases and useful illustrations come back to mind. The traffic between the written and the spoken word flows in both directions, for experience of what concerns people, learned from discussion times, can guide the choice of future writing topics.

*I need a computer to translate my illegible handwriting into readable form,
but I continue to resist e-mail as a form of communication*

When I began to write about science and religion in a sustained and systematic way, I had to decide what was to be my principal audience, the academy or the general educated public. In either case, I would need to write as truthfully and carefully as I could, but the style of presentation would be different in the two cases. In academic writing, you have to itemize detail in as full and scrupulous a way as possible and you are comparatively free to use technical terms in doing so. The general reader, on the other hand, requires a treatment that is careful and clear about concepts and conclusions, but which does not need to be documented in terms of extensively footnoted minutiae. Any technical terms that are used will need to be explained. I had experience of both these styles of writing in my physics days. The two professional monographs with which I had been associated were stylistically quite different from my semi-popular writings about particle physics and quantum theory. I decided that the readership that I was principally called to address in this new phase of authorship was made up of believers and honest enquirers rather than simply professional scholars, though I hoped that the latter would nevertheless be able to find relevant material of interest in what I wrote. The possibility of being able at least partially to address both kinds of audience was encouraged by the interdisciplinary character of the subject material. Theological readers would not have professional knowledge of the scientific ideas that I needed to use, while scientists would not have much prior acquaintance with the results of biblical scholarship and the insights of systematic theology that were also necessary for the discussion. There would be very few readers equally at home in both fields. Of course, that applied to the author as well. I knew that I did not straddle the frontier between science and theology with my feet equally firmly planted on both sides of the border. I have a serious interest in theology and read as much professional writing on the subject as I can. Yet life is not long enough to serve twice the long apprenticeship to learning that is required if one is to become a professional scholar. I remain a theoretical physicist who has a strong but essentially amateur concern with matters theological, rather than a bilingual professional equally fluent in both disciplines. Interdisciplinary activity necessarily requires a degree of intellectual boldness (for one has to venture into fields of knowledge of which one is not totally the master) and a degree of intellectual charity (for everyone starts from one side or the other of the frontier and needs help and encouragement from those on the other side). I believe that the demands and risks of interdisciplinarity are made worthwhile by the reward it brings in terms of an extended insight. I often say of myself that I strive to be two-eyed, looking with both the eye of science and with the eye of religion, and that such binocular vision enables me to see more than would be possible with either eye on its own. When I write, and especially when I speak, I feel I have a double mission: on the one hand to encourage scientists to take religion seriously and not dismiss it unreflectively without a hearing, and on the other hand to encourage religious people to take science seriously and not to fear the truth that it brings.

Neither science nor religion can pretend to answer the other's questions direct. Each has its own proper domain of enquiry. Roughly speaking, science addresses the question of the processes by which things happen. It seeks answers by means of the experimental interrogation of an objective dimension of reality which is open to manipulative investigation, repeatable as often as necessary. Roughly speaking, religion addresses the question of whether there is meaning and purpose present in what is happening. Its answers arise principally out of encounters with personal reality and from reflection on the unique record of particular disclosures of the transpersonal reality of God, that theology calls revelation. In this domain of experience, testing has to give way to trusting. Different though the two kinds of rational enquiry are from each other, nevertheless there must be a harmonious relationship between the insights of science and religion if it is the case that both are offering perspectives onto the one world of reality. Hence the need for a dialogue between them, a conversation whose principal goal is the quest for consonance as, for example, when one considers how the insights of evolutionary biology and creation theology properly relate to each other.

It grieves me when some religious people refuse the insights that science can offer into the structure of the physical world and the history of life within it. It grieves me also when some scientists scorn religion, using against it arguments that exhibit a degree of theological naivety comparable to the scientific naivety of people who write papers with titles such as 'Einstein was Wrong'.

I believe that the style that I adopted as a consequence of my decision about what should be my principal target audience has occasionally resulted in some academic readers not recognizing that accessibility need not be purchased at the cost of conceptual carefulness. Certainly I always seek to write with intellectual scrupulosity. Later, as I give some account of my individual writings, I shall say something about my contributions to the long discussion about the question of divine action that occupied the science and theology community to such a great extent in the 1990s. At that time, I was quite often irritated by what I saw as the inability of some of my colleagues to have the courtesy to read carefully what I had actually written on these issues. From the start I had recognized the elementary philosophical point that there is a critical distinction between epistemology (what can be known) and ontology (what is the case). In fact it is one of the most important issues in philosophy – and perhaps the most important issue in the philosophy of science – what connection should be postulated between them, asserted as a matter of metaphysical decision. I had explicitly explained that I adopted the realist strategy of aligning the two as closely as possible. Yet I was sometimes treated as if I were unaware of this issue, or had not addressed it. This attitude was particularly galling since it usually came from those who blithely assumed that quantum theory is unproblematically causally open, a metaphysical position that requires exactly the same kind of analysis and defence that I was prepared to give in my explorations of the use of chaos theory.

I write reasonably concisely, in a style that comes naturally to a scientist. We say what we want to say, without rhetorical embroidery, and then finish. A reviewer once compared a book of mine to the Tardis (a science-fiction machine belonging to the timelord Dr Who, which on the outside appears to be a police phone box, but which on the inside proves to have sufficient room to house an elaborate machine for time-travel). This image of *multum in parvo*, small without but spacious within, pleased me. I write short books, but try to fill them with ideas, both those of others and those that are my own. I also like to revisit topics after a few years when my thoughts have developed a bit more, in a kind of spiralling process that seeks at each turn to move closer to the heart of the matter, without simply repeating what had been said before. The result of these authorial habits has been quite a large number of fairly short books, rather than a few *magna opera*. The latter writing strategy has been the more common one among contemporary scientist-theologians, such as Ian Barbour and Arthur Peacocke. It is, of course, undeniably convenient to be able to find much of a person's thought between the covers of one or two large books, and I realize that my approach makes more demands upon the persistence of someone seeking an adequate view of my thinking. I hope that the overview of my theological writings that follows will not only provide a sketch of my thought for a general reader, but it will also be of some help to anyone wanting to take a careful look into my total contribution to the dialogue between science and theology. Certainly such a person would need to be prepared to read more than a couple of books. I believe that my chosen strategy has been the right one for me to follow. With so much exploration recently going on across the frontier between science and religion, I consider that it has been appropriate to cast what I want to say partially in the episodic mode of reports of continuing work in progress.

I also know that at least some of my readers appreciate brevity. It will also be apparent that the small-book strategy has enabled me to write at a number of intellectual levels, something which is not too common in the science and religion world, but which I value.

While I had been Vicar in the Blean, I had written *One World: The interaction of science and theology*, published in 1986. Its reception was encouraging and it sold quite well (it has recently returned to print). No doubt sales had been favourably influenced by a short radio talk given by a leading British theologian, Keith Ward. At that time, the BBC had a five-minute slot on a Sunday morning in which a speaker gave a brief account of a recently published religious book. One Sunday, Keith chose to talk about *One World* and he did so in a welcoming way. Looking at the book again today, I am struck by how many themes it contains, even if treated in brief, that were to prove recurrent concerns given further and more developed treatment in my subsequent writings. In the book, science and theology are compared and, despite their obviously different subject material, both are held to be concerned with the search for truthful understanding, pursued through the formulation of well-motivated beliefs. These two forms of rational enquiry are shown to inter-relate through their giving complementary accounts of cosmic history, which is interpretable both from the perspective of physical process and from the perspective of belief in the purposes of a Creator. There is no direct entailment between these two approaches, but their insights must bear some sort of consonant relationship to each other. A revised form of natural theology is proposed, not seeking to rival science on its own explanatory ground, but taking the laws of nature that science has to treat as simply given brute fact and setting them in a more profound context of understanding. Thus the deep rational transparency of the universe, that gives science its opportunity, and the profound rational beauty of that universe's fundamental structure, which gives scientists the experience of wonder as the reward for their labours, are not just treated as if they were happy accidents. Rather, they are made intelligible by being understood as signs of the divine Mind that lies behind the order of the world. The insights of the anthropic principle into the remarkable fine-tuning of the quantitative character of the laws of nature, which was indispensable if the universe were ever to be capable of evolving carbon-based life anywhere within it, can be removed from the category of happy accident by being interpreted as a divine endowment expressive of the Creator's fruitful purpose. Christian claims of miracle are not to be understood as referring to the acts of a capricious celestial conjurer, but they are the record of unique events which provide more profound insight into the divine nature than that which is discernible through routine experience. Miracles, such as the resurrection of Christ, afford access to a deepened understanding of God, much in the way that a new physical regime (such as subatomic physics) can open up a window into novel and surprising aspects of the character of physical process. As a whole, the book was intended, as its title suggests, to defend my deep conviction of the essential unity of knowledge, a belief underwritten in my mind by the unity of the God who is the ground of all that exists. The book was dedicated to my friends in the Society of the Sacred Cross at Tymawr Convent.

I then wrote *Science and Creation: The search for understanding*, based on some invited lectures given in the University of Dundee and published in 1988. It contains further reflections on natural theology and on the doctrine of creation. In the formulation of the latter, science's evolutionary insights encourage the recognition that creation is not a single once-for-all act, but the unfolding of a continuous process, a point that had been particularly emphasized by my friend and colleague, Arthur Peacocke. One chapter explores, necessarily in a tentative way, a concept of the nature of created reality that sees the material and the mental as being complementary aspects of a single 'world stuff', rather than as two distinct substances in the manner of Plato or Descartes. I believe that human beings are psychosomatic unities, rather than apprentice angels whose separable spiritual nature awaits release at death from the encumbrance of a fleshly body. This is an idea which would neither have surprised nor shocked the writers of the Bible, for Hebrew thought took just such a 'package deal' view of human nature.

A third volume, *Science and Providence: God's interaction with the world*, appeared in 1989. Much of what had been said about natural theology, or even about creation, was as consistent with the distant and spectatorial god of deism, who simply set the universe going and then let it all happen, as it was with the God of theism, providentially active within creation's history. Yet it is the latter God who is the subject of the belief of the three great Abrahamic faiths, Judaism, Christianity and Islam. Prayer is surely more than a rhetorical exercise in self-assurance, and it is more fitting to call God 'Father' rather than 'Force', not because anyone thinks that God is an old man in the sky, but simply because we believe that God is more like a personal Agent who does particular things on particular occasions, rather than like gravity which is unchanging in its effects.

But is it possible both to believe in such providential divine action and also to take absolutely seriously what science tells us about the regularity of the laws of nature? If science's picture were that of a merely mechanical universe, I do not think that this would be possible. However, twentieth-century science saw the death of mere mechanism through the discovery of widespread intrinsic unpredictabilities present in nature, revealed first at the subatomic level of quantum theory, and then at the everyday level of chaos theory. What this might imply for the actual causal structure of the world requires further metascientific argument. While science constrains our ideas about causality, it is insufficient of itself to determine them completely. Unpredictability is an epistemological property (you cannot know about future behaviour), but this ignorance might be due to a variety of different possible reasons: either a lack of access to the detail of some causal factors or the presence of a genuine degree of openness to the future. I have already declared my realist philosophical convictions, affirming that what we know, or cannot know, should be treated as a reliable guide to what is the case. (Ruth once gave me a sweat-shirt inscribed with the stirring motto, 'Epistemology models Ontology', words that she had often heard me utter as a slogan expression of the realist position.) The realist will see intrinsic unpredictabilities as being signs of a genuine ontological openness, not meaning by this that the future is the result of some random lottery, but that more causal principles are at work to bring it about than simply the conventional scientific reductionist account of the exchange of energy between constituents. In *Science and Providence* I made this point about there being an opportunity for a metascientific decision about the character of causality, but I put it in so brief a form that I now recognize that it was insufficiently clearly presented. It was scarcely surprising that not all readers took it on board at that time. More writing on this issue was soon to come, in which I would be careful to make the point much more explicitly.

I believe that the extra causal principles arising in this way include those that allow human beings to act as agents in the world. When I raise my arm there is, of course, a bits-and-pieces aspect to what is happening, as currents flow in nerves, and muscles contract. But also it is I, the whole person, who is exercising the power of intentional action. If I can act in this way in a world of becoming that is open to its future, I see no reason to suppose that God, that world's Creator, cannot also act providentially in some analogous way within the course of its history. Theological thinking about divine action has to avoid two unacceptable extremes: the Cosmic Tyrant who does everything and allows no independent power at all to creatures, and the Deistic Spectator who just stands aside and lets it all happen. The Christian God is the God of love who neither abandons creatures nor prevents them from being themselves and 'making themselves' – the latter phrase being the theological way to interpret the scientific insight of the evolutionary processes by which potentiality is explored and brought to actuality. According to this view, God interacts with creatures but does not over-rule the gift of due independence which they have been given. In this understanding there lies some degree of answer to the problem of the evil and suffering present in creation.

The free-will defence in relation to moral evil (human acts of cruelty or neglect) asserts that it is a greater good to have a world populated with freely choosing moral beings, rather than a world of perfectly programmed automata. One cannot say those words after the twentieth century without a quiver in the voice, but I believe it to be a true insight, however difficult to embrace. I suggested that one needs to add to that insight a free-process defence in relation to natural evil (disease and disaster), asserting the greater good of a world in which fruitfulness arises through the evolutionary exploration of potentiality, compared with a world of ready-made rigid necessity. An evolving creation of that kind must inescapably have its shadow side, for its processes will have blind alleys and ragged edges as well as great triumphs of fertility. I believe that God wills directly neither the act of a murderer nor the devastation wrought by an earthquake, but both are permitted to happen in a world that is more than a divine puppet theatre. The act of creation has been what the theologians call a kenotic act, a divine self-limitation of power in order to allow creatures to be themselves and to make themselves.

There is a further theological insight about creation that is more contentious, but which I also believe is true. According to this view, the creation of a world of real becoming is understood to have involved a kenotic self-limitation of divine knowledge. Even God does not yet know the unformed future, for it is not yet there to be known, though undoubtedly God sees much more clearly than any creature can the general way in which history is moving. Taking this point of view implies that the eternal God, in bringing a temporal world into being, has condescended also to engage with the reality of time. This dipolar, eternity/temporality concept of God's nature has been an important ingredient in much contemporary theology.

I wrote *Science and Providence* to explore all these issues, at least in a preliminary way, because I believed that the next major item in the agenda for science and religion would be taking the discussion beyond the consideration of properties simply consistent with the static god of deism, in order that the discourse might engage with the dynamic God of theism. This expectation was fully confirmed by the sustained wrestling with questions of divine action that occupied so much of the attention of the science and theology community in the 1990s. These three books that I had written, *One World*, *Science and Creation* and *Science and Providence*, constituted an inter-related trilogy forming the first cycle of my spiral exploration of science and religion.

In 1991 I published *Reason and Reality: The relationship between science and religion*, intended as the first arc of a new and tighter cycle of exploration. I gave a more detailed discussion of critical realism and I explained how I use concepts such as models, metaphor and theory, in what I believe to be a more discriminatory manner than some other writers. I defended a theological concept of divine revelation, understood as referring to particular unique moments of God's self-disclosure, together with the record given in scripture of these events, rather than its involving some ineffable communication of propositional dogma. For Christian theology, revelatory significance is specially to be found in the history of Israel and in the life, death and resurrection of Jesus Christ. I wrote a chapter which gave a much clearer and more explicit account of my ideas about physical causality in relation to human and divine agency. Without neglecting a possible role for quantum theory, I laid particular stress on the promise of the unpredictabilities present in chaos theory, since they are directly relevant to the kind of macroscopic phenomena that appear likely to be significant for agential action. I also devoted the last chapter of the book to a new topic for me, how to interpret the Adam and Eve story of Genesis 3, in order to understand rightly the theological concept of the Fall. Read at a superficially literal level, this powerful ancient story is irreconcilable with what science tells us about the past history of life and the development of hominids. To deal with this we need to take its mythic character seriously, not meaning that it is to be treated as a worn-out fable that we can readily discard, but that it conveys in story form an insight into that almost unimaginable (but indubitable) event, the dawning of hominid self-consciousness. The power thus gained to project human thought into the future, even to the extent of foreseeing the inevitability of eventual death, would also, I believe, have been accompanied by a dawning consciousness of the presence of God. The Fall was the process, of which we are still the heirs, by which our ancestors then turned away from God and into themselves. This did not bring biological death into the world, for that had already been there for many millions of years, but it did bring what one might venture to call 'mortality', human sadness and bitterness at the recognition of the transience of life, felt forcibly by those who had divorced themselves from the God whose faithfulness is the only true ground of the hope of a destiny beyond death.

A year or two previously, I had been invited to give the Gifford Lectures at Edinburgh University in the academic year 1993–4. The opportunity offered is one that is expected to be treated with considerable seriousness, and so one is given long notice in order to have time for extensive preparation. Not only was I honoured by the invitation, but it was a particular pleasure for me that in delivering the lectures I would be returning to the university in which I had begun my teaching career. The Gifford Lectures, which take place in the four ancient Scottish universities, were intended by Lord Gifford to be concerned with 'The Knowledge of God', treated by those who aspire to be 'sincere lovers of and enquirers after truth'. The lecturers are bidden not to appeal to any unquestionable source of propositional revelation, but they are to engage in 'Promoting, Advancing, Teaching and Diffusing the study of Natural Theology'. I chose to concentrate nine out of my ten lectures on the discussion and defence of clauses drawn from the Nicene Creed. One might reasonably ask how was this approach held to be consistent with the founder's wishes? The essence of my answer is to be found in the subtitle of the published version of the lectures, which is 'Theological Reflections of a Bottom-up Thinker'.

The natural inclination of a scientist is not to ask about a truth claim, 'Is it reasonable?', as if we knew beforehand what shape rationality had to take. The physical world has proved to be too strange beyond our prior expectation for that to be appropriate. Quantum theory makes the

A bottom-up thinker

point clearly enough. The natural question for the scientist is somewhat different, 'What makes you think that might be the case?' This manner of enquiry does not pre-judge what form the answer ought to take, but evidence is demanded for what is being asserted. I call this type of approach 'bottom-up thinking'. It starts in the basement of experience and then seeks to move up to the ground floor of understanding, in contrast to top-down thinking, which believes it can start on the tenth floor of general and self-evident principles before descending to the consideration of particulars. The trouble with the latter strategy is that the principles appealed to have so often proved to be neither general nor self-evident.

I must confess that quite often when I read works of philosophical theology or of the philosophy of science, I am troubled by the highly generalized tone of much of the discourse. It seems to me that the arguments require earthing in detailed consideration of specific revelatory events (in the case of theology) or in specific episodes of investigation and discovery (in the case of science). Of course there is scope for the proposal and evaluation of overarching principles, bringing together sets of specific insights under more general modes of understanding, but it seems to me that this should come at the end, rather than at the beginning, of the discussion.

In my Giffords I wanted to be able to approach theology in a bottom-up spirit similar to that in which I approach science. To do so would, I hoped, show some of my scientific colleagues, who are wary of religion because they think it is based on an unquestioning submission to an unchallengeable authority, that they could engage with Christianity without the fear of being exhorted to commit intellectual suicide. Faith truly seeks understanding through motivated belief. The argument, given in the nine chapters of my Gifford Lectures that concentrated on claims made in the Nicene Creed, was set out in precisely the manner of such a search for well-motivated belief. I believe that Lord Gifford would have found this strategy an acceptable use of his endowment. To give an example, a pivotal issue for Christian belief is the resurrection of Jesus Christ. His earthly life seems to end in ambiguity and failure: deserted by his followers, subjected to a shameful and painful death of a kind that any first-century Jew would have regarded as a sign of God's rejection, with a cry of dereliction, 'My God, my God, why have you forsaken me?', on his lips. I honestly believe that if the story of Jesus had ended there, he would have had no impact on history. Yet all have heard of Jesus and he has been one of the most influential figures in the history of the world. Something happened to continue the story. After a careful sifting of the New Testament evidence, I find myself persuaded to accept the explanation offered by its writers, that God did indeed raise Jesus from the dead the first Easter Day, however counterintuitive such a belief might at first sight seem to be.

The tenth lecture was concerned with a different topic, one that has long exercised and perplexed me. The acceptance of science is world-wide. Ask suitably qualified people in London, Delhi or Tokyo what nuclear matter is made of, and in all three cities you will receive the same answer: quarks and gluons. Ask three people in the same three cities what is the nature of ultimate reality, and you may expect to receive three very different answers. This degree of religious cognitive clash is disturbing, not least to scientifically minded people, conscious of the universality achieved by their own discipline. The diversity of the world faith traditions is a pressing problem that I expect to be high on the theological agenda not only for the twenty-first century, but for the whole of the third millennium. All traditions preserve and nurture genuine spiritual experience, but they say conflicting things about its fundamental character. Of course there are overlaps (for instance, in the value given to compassion and in the accounts given of the unitive character of mystical encounter), but simply compiling a lowest-common-denominator account seems to me to yield too etiolated a description of religion to be satisfactory. Long and painful dialogue between the faiths lies ahead. They will need initially to discuss together issues that are serious but not so mutually challenging that defences immediately go up all round. One such issue could be how the faiths relate the insights of modern science to their foundational traditions.

My Gifford Lectures were published in 1994. I made the mistake, which I subsequently came to regret, of allowing them to appear under different titles on the two sides of the Atlantic: *Science and Christian Belief* in Britain, and *The Faith of a Physicist* in North America. I have had American friends who, having read the American edition, came to Britain and bought what they thought was a new title, only to find its contents strangely familiar. I must admit, however, that the title chosen by my transatlantic publishers now seems to me to have been the better one.

It had been hard work preparing for the Giffords. After they had been delivered, I decided that I needed a short holiday from academic endeavour. Since I like to keep writing, I turned my hand to producing a little book that would survey the science and religion scene in a responsible way, but without excess of detail. After giving a public lecture, I had quite often been approached by someone from the audience who asked me to recommend a book of mine for them to read. Frequently it was clear that what they wanted was something covering the ground, but not in too specialized a manner. With such enquirers I had not known quite what to recommend, so now I decided to write a book that would meet their need. The result was *Quarks, Chaos and Christianity* (1994). It was fun to write – I could do so out of my head without the need for extensive reading around – and I have to say that I am rather fond of the result. In terms of BBC radio, I regard it as my 'Radio 4' book, while most of my other writing is 'Radio 3' in character. (Radio 4 is general public broadcasting, while Radio 3 is rather more for people with intellectual inclinations.) Best of all, people quite often tell me that they have enjoyed the book and found it helpful. It appeared in an updated edition in 2005.

Next I was persuaded to assemble some lectures I had given on various occasions to form *Serious Talk: Science and religion in dialogue* (1995). The book has the character of a survey of my thinking up to that point, rather than the presentation of totally new material. Perhaps its most useful contribution is given in two chapters that present eight-point accounts of science and religion, laid out in a manner that brings out the similarities between these two truth-seeking endeavours.

A different kind of writing resulted from an invitation from the Bible Reading Fellowship to be the author of their Lent Book for 1997. I produced *Searching for Truth: A scientist looks at the Bible*. Scripture is very important to me in my own Christian life, and as an Anglican priest saying the Daily Office I read through a good deal of the Bible every year, including the whole of the New Testament. The format that I chose for the Lent Book was the traditional one of selecting a passage of scripture for each of the 40 days, writing a short comment on it drawing out something of its significance for Christian living, and concluding with a short prayer. Each week had an over-riding theme, varying from Creation to Suffering. The conciseness required suited my style. I was grateful for the invitation and really enjoyed the task.

There has been a vast amount of writing on science and religion over the last 20 years, but comparatively little of it has been devoted to producing secondary literature. By that term I mean books that do not simply put forward their author's own views, but which seek to cover the thought of several leading figures, describing their insights in a comparative way that brings out the significance both of agreements and differences. I decided eventually that I would try my hand at writing such a book myself. The project I had in mind was based on analysing the work of three authors, scientist-theologians who had written extensively and influentially in the area of science and religion. One of these authors was Ian Barbour, the doyen of our field, whose book *Issues in Science and Religion* (1966) had been a seminal volume. Ian has consistently attached importance to employing the resources of process theology, based on the ideas of Alfred North Whitehead, one of the most creative philosophers of the twentieth century. For Whitehead the fundamental category of reality is event ('an actual occasion'), which has a 'prehensive' phase in which past events and future possibilities act as influences, followed by a 'concrescent' phase in which a particular outcome occurs. God acts through a persuasive lure in the first phase, but the selection of the final consequence lies with the event itself, a notion that gives a panpsychic tinge to process thinking. I personally find a number of serious difficulties, both philosophical and theological, with process thought, but Barbour, while acknowledging the need for some degree of revision, has made it central to his own thinking. My second author was Arthur Peacocke, like myself an Anglican priest, whose scientific experience had been in biology and who had written very helpfully about how to understand evolutionary processes theologically, interpreted as the means of an unfolding act of continuous creation. The third author was myself. I had to acknowledge that this last choice made comparative analysis a delicate matter, but I was greatly helped by my two colleagues who kindly read and commented on an early draft of the manuscript, though the responsibility for what was actually published lay, of course, with me alone.

The resulting volume, *Scientists as Theologians: A comparison of the writings of Ian Barbour, Arthur Peacocke and John Polkinghorne*, was published in 1996. In it I classified strategies for pursuing a dialogue between science and religion in terms of varying degrees of searching for consonance (the mutual congruence of the two perspectives afforded by science and theology) and for assimilation (the achievement of a measure of fusion of the two modes of thought). Barbour was placed towards the assimilation end of the spectrum, since process thinking attempts just such an integration. Peacocke was somewhere in the middle, and I put myself clearly towards the consonance end. Later I came to feel that a different mode of analysis was required, placing emphasis on content rather than on method, as I shall describe in due course. One significant matter of theological content that was addressed in the 1996 book was the issue of panentheism. This theological stance must be distinguished clearly from pantheism. The latter equates God and the world, but panentheism asserts that, though the world is held to be in God in some sense, God nevertheless exceeds the world. Barbour and Peacocke both inclined to panentheistic views, but I adhered to the more classical Christian understanding that maintains a clear distinction between Creator and creation, while acknowledging that God's relationship to creatures has the character of immanence as well as transcendence. Any blurring of the line between Creator and creation seems to me to intensify the problem of evil and suffering.

Yet another book published in 1996 was *Beyond Science: The wider human context*. Its style of presentation was secular rather than theological, as it sought to place scientific insight and experience within a wider context of humane, metaphysical and ethical understanding. I also included in it some brief reminiscences of famous physicists whom I had known.

Quite a lot of my writing has been the fruit of invitations to give endowed lectures at various universities. I was honoured to be asked to give the Terry Lectures at Yale, and pleased to be given a fairly free choice of when to do so. Ruth and I had always wanted to see New England in the Fall, and so I asked for my lectures to be scheduled for two weeks in the middle of October 1996, just after I had retired. We were very hospitably received and we very much enjoyed exploring the Yale campus and being taken on drives through the brightly coloured autumn landscape. The lectures were published in 1998 by Yale University Press as *Belief in God in an Age of Science*. This was the beginning of what has proved to be a long and pleasant association with the Yale Press, who have been the North American publishers of several of my books. I took the opportunity to dedicate *Belief in God* to the Society for Promoting Christian Knowledge, on the occasion of its tercentenary, for SPCK has been my principal British publisher for a very long time, a connection also much valued by me.

Belief in God represented another turn in the exploratory spiral. Its opening chapter presents an extended concept of natural theology, going beyond recourse to science's insights into the order and fertility of the physical world to include an appeal to the existence of value, both aesthetic and moral, seen as an irreducibly significant dimension in our encounter with reality, and laying emphasis on the significance of the human instinct of hope. The following chapter contains a detailed five-point comparison between the search for insight in quantum physics and the search for insight in Christology. Another chapter defends critical realism in both science and theology, making its argument by drawing on particular illustrations selected from these two forms of rational enquiry. In accordance with my bottom-up thinking, I believe that a critical realist position must draw its persuasiveness from the consideration of particular instances, rather than attempting to rely on a top-down appeal to general principles. Yet another chapter gives a careful account of what I understand about the relationship of theories of divine action to the insights of contemporary science. In terms of sales, the book has proved to be one of the most successful of my writings on science and religion.

Many university and college courses on science and religion had come into being in the previous few years, often encouraged by generous initial support offered by the John Templeton Foundation. I decided that I would like to make a contribution to this activity by writing a book that could be used as a textbook. *Science and Theology: An introduction* (1998) was, in effect, a more academically oriented version of *Quarks,*

Chaos and Christianity, as well as making a further contribution to the secondary literature. The material used was derived principally from my experience of teaching a semester course as a visiting professor at General Theological Seminary in New York City, following my retirement from Queens'. The book seeks to concentrate succinctly on key issues and to give an account that acknowledges the contributions of a variety of different authors and contrasting strategies.

Another North American association that has proved to have been particularly important for me, has been an extended connection with the Center of Theological Inquiry (CTI) at Princeton. One of the activities of the Center has been the organization and support of theological consultations, involving 15 to 20 people meeting twice a year for three years or so, in order to pursue research together into some specific theological topic. I have been involved successively in three such consultations. The first concerned divine action, including a particular concentration on the question of God's relationship to time. A paper that I wrote for those meetings subsequently became a chapter in *Faith, Science and Understanding*, published in 2000. Unlike most of my books, this one did not have a single unifying theme, but its material broke up into three somewhat separate sections: the first giving some general thoughts about science and religion issues, including a defence of the necessary role of a theological department in a complete university; the second continuing the discussion of divine agency and including a chapter that surveyed and critiqued four different schemes for the relationship of God to time; the third looking at the work on science and religion of three significant thinkers. Two of these were distinguished theologians, Wolfhart Pannenberg and Thomas Torrance, while the third was Paul Davies, an extensive and successful writer of books on science for the general reader. Two of his books had invoked some concept of the Mind of God, used as an expression of the author's conviction that science on its own is not enough to provide an intellectually satisfying account of what is going on in the universe. Davies stands outside any religious tradition, and he is an interesting illustration both of the possibility of a stand-alone natural theology, and also of the relative poverty of that position when it is divorced from other sources of theological insight.

At CTI, one of my colleagues with whom I had felt a special affinity was a German systematic theologian from Heidelberg, Michael Welker. We have become close friends and I have gained much theological understanding from our many conversations. Together we organized the second CTI consultation of which I was a member. Its topic was eschatology, the theological discussion of questions of ultimate destiny, both for human beings and for the whole created cosmos. We know that we are going to die, and the cosmologists reliably inform us that the universe itself will eventually die, most probably through becoming too cold and too dilute to sustain life anywhere within it. What do these prognostications imply for the religious claim that the world is God's creation, if in the end all is futility? Christian theology speaks of a destiny beyond death, a hope based on the faithfulness of God and the resurrection of Jesus Christ. Can one make sense today of such an ancient hope? If one is to do so, it soon becomes clear that there is need to appeal to both continuity (so that individuals truly live again and are not just new characters given the old names) and discontinuity (so that people are not simply made alive again in order to die again). A group of theologians, scientists and other scholars wrestled with these issues at CTI, and our contributions were eventually published as *The End of the World and the Ends of God: Science and theology on eschatology* (2000), edited by Michael and myself. As this work was being completed, the group recognized that the papers in our joint volume were likely to prove fairly demanding for many readers. It was suggested that a single-author volume, covering the field in a careful but less academically detailed way, might also be desirable. I like that sort of writing, and so, with the encouragement of my colleagues, I went on to write *The God of Hope and the End of the World* (2002). It is not a digest of the earlier book, for I organized the material in my own way and expressed my own opinions and ideas, but it did draw much inspiration from our work together. The third consultation at CTI of which I have been a member was concerned with theological anthropology and it resulted in the publication of *God and Human Dignity*, edited by Kendall Soulen and Linda Woodhead.

I have also been able to write a book for the seasons of Advent and Christmas, laid out in a format similar to that of my Lent Book, which offers access to eschatological insights in the form of 'bite-sized' daily portions. It appeared in 2003, entitled *Living with Hope: A scientist looks at Advent, Christmas and Epiphany*, and it covers such topics as the Four Last Things (death, judgement, heaven, hell) and the Incarnation.

In the meantime, I had become associated with two other books. One was written with Michael Welker, *Faith in the Living God – A dialogue* (2001). It arose from a long visit I paid to Heidelberg, generously financed by a prize grant from the Alexander von Humboldt Foundation. Michael and I taught a joint course on the fundamentals of Christian belief, and the resulting book covers topics such as Faith in God the Creator, Faith in Christ, Faith in the Holy Spirit. We each present our personal understanding of these matters, the other responds with comments, and the original author then adds a final word. I believe the result to be a lively dialogue between two very different people, a German reformed theologian and a British Anglican physicist, about the fundamental Christian convictions that they both share.

In 1998 I had organized a meeting, supported by the Templeton Foundation and held in Queens', at which a number of scientists and theologians met to discuss the doctrine of creation, understood in the light of a kenotic understanding of God's relationship with creatures. After a further meeting to tie up loose ends, our papers were published in 2001 as *The Work of Love: Creation as kenosis*, which I had edited. It gives a multi-perspectival account of what has surely been one of the twentieth century's most promising developments in theology.

These writings, and particularly the work on eschatology, were signs of the presence of an increasingly more serious theological component in the dialogue between science and religion. The spiral of exploration was tightening and moving closer to the heart of the matter, as theology came to play a greater part in setting the agenda. This increase in theological intensity has been reflected in my own writing. Recently, I have

Five Templeton Prize winners (me, Arthur Peacocke, George Ellis,
Michael Bourdeaux and Sigmund Sternberg)

sought to make much more use of trinitarian insight than I had done
previously. There has been encouragement for this approach from the
perception of a complementary increase in scientific recognition of the
importance of relationality in our understanding of the physical world,
whether from discoveries concerning quantum entanglement that show
how quantum entities can remain causally intimate despite spatial
separation, or from the integrative insights of general relativity which
combine space, time and matter in a single package deal, or from the
holistic self-organizing properties found to be possessed by complex
systems. These scientific ideas are certainly consonant with the Christian
belief that the Creator of all reality is also relational in character. The
Christian concept of God is the trinitarian picture of the mutual and
unending exchange of love between the three divine Persons, Father,
Son and Holy Spirit, united in the single life of the Godhead.

Two recent books, *Science and the Trinity: The Christian encounter with reality* (2004) and *Exploring Reality: The intertwining of science and religion* (2005) have both focused on taking a trinitarian approach to issues of science and religion. They also return to, and extend, previous discussions of topics such as scripture, the historical Jesus, and the Eucharist, thereby representing another turn in my spiral engagement with science and religion. *Science and the Trinity* also contains a chapter in which I seek to classify participants in the science and religion dialogue in terms of the character and scope of the theological content of their writing. Four categories are employed. Paul Davies exemplifies a deistic approach, since his picture of God does not amount to much more than the source of cosmic order. Ian Barbour exemplifies an approach that I labelled as theistic. While Barbour's writing is clearly Christian in its basic character, it does not seem to me to pay sufficient attention to some important Nicene topics, such as the resurrection. Arthur Peacocke exemplifies a position that one may call revisionary, since in his last writings he began to call for changes in traditional understandings to an extent that I personally did not regard as being demanded by contemporary scientific insights. My own stance I call developmental. Each generation has to make Christian truth its own in its own way, and the manner of doing this will be influenced by scientific advances, but I believe that one can interpret the process as being exploration conducted in a recognizably continuous relationship to the insights of past generations.

In addition to further trinitarian discussion, *Exploring Reality* has a chapter in which I consider humanity in the context of its evolutionary origin, arguing that the multi-levelled character of human beings only becomes intelligible if the environment in which they have evolved is recognized as exceeding in richness and depth the simple physico–biological world of conventional Darwinian orthodoxy. Another chapter makes it clear how open and patchy, in fact, is science's account of the causal structure of the world. For example, quantum theory (which has an intrinsic scale set by Planck's constant) and chaos theory (whose fractal character implies that it is scale-free) cannot consistently be reconciled with each other. A new feature in my writing is a chapter devoted to ethical issues, centring on questions arising from recent advances in human genetics. I indicate my belief that the evaluation of the moral status of the very early embryo depends critically on whether one takes a dualist or psychosomatic view of human nature.

My most recent book is *Quantum Physics and Theology: An unexpected kinship* (2007). It pursues in great detail the similarities I discern between the truth-seeking strategies employed in physics and in theology, basing the argument in a bottom-up fashion on an analysis of 14 paired occasions of discovery and enhanced insight in the two disciplines. I believe that these examples display methodological parallels that strongly encourage the discernment of an intellectual kinship between science and theology, a relationship that can only be established by the study of particular examples, rather than by an attempt at generalized argument.

A number of my books have appeared in translation. The linguistic range covered by these different versions stretches, all in all, over 18 different languages, but there is one notable gap. I have never had a book translated into French. This may reflect not only a certain Gallic reserve about Anglo-Saxon thinking in general, but also that my sort of concise style is, perhaps, not congenial to French taste. Nevertheless, I entertain a secret hope that one day this gap might be filled.

Finally, I should mention two of my short books, or long pamphlets, which are more likely to be found on bookstalls in churches and retreat houses than in academic bookshops. One is *Traffic in Truth: Exchanges between science and theology* (2000), written for the Sisters at Tymawr and which gives a short introduction to its topic woven around a sustained metaphor of life on a frontier, an approach appropriate to the Convent's setting near the border between England and Wales. The other is *The Archbishop's School of Christianity and Science* (2003), one of a series of aids to Christian life and thought produced under the patronage of David Hope when he was Archbishop of York.

I have always liked to try new forms of writing, and this autobiographical essay is a further experiment in the pleasant occupation of being an author.

16

Committees

Given its title, it is scarcely likely that this chapter will excite in many readers a sense of the eager expectation of a thrilling read. Aren't committees just boring but unavoidable aspects of modern life? Certainly there can be *longueurs* in committee work, but if sensible and agreed decisions are to be made with the adequate participation of knowledgeable and interested parties, something like committee meetings seems to be the best way of achieving this desirable end. I have usually enjoyed the discussions themselves. Where the work has sometimes been burdensome has been in the weight of paper one had to read in preparation for the meeting. I have been involved in a good number of committees of various kinds and an account of my life that omitted this aspect of it altogether would be incomplete.

It is often the case that the most desirable seat at a committee is in the chair. Occupying it will involve extra work and responsibility, but one is given the opportunity to steer the business and to give some guidance about decisions. I have already said, in relation to committee life in College, that the person who is in the chair needs to have at least a provisional idea of how the discussion might end. Some of my most frustrating hours of committee work have been spent in circumstances where the person presiding seemed to have no such notion, lacking the resolve to put the question and simply letting the discussion circle round and round the proverbial mulberry bush.

It would be intolerably tedious to attempt to list the many committees on which I have served and the many decisions that they needed to make. I shall be content to illustrate my experience by selecting some specimen examples drawn from the three broad types of committee of which I have been a member: academic, governmental and ecclesiastical.

Cambridge University has three principal central committees: the General Board (academic policy), the Council of the Senate (broad responsibilities within the life of the University), and the Financial Board (expenditure and resources, both monetary and bricks and mortar). Meetings are presided over by the Vice-Chancellor and they are conducted with some degree of formality. Gowns are worn; at every meeting one sits at the same assigned place around the table; everyone rises when the Vice-Chancellor enters and leaves and he/she is addressed formally throughout the proceedings. In the course of my career I served on all three of these central bodies. First I did a normal four-year stint on the General Board while I was still a professor in DAMTP. During the second half of this period I was Chairman of the Board's Work and Stipends Committee, concerned with issues related to terms of employment. The biggest issue on the agenda of the General Board itself, for most of my service on it, was the setting up of a full-blown medical school, based principally at Addenbrookes Hospital. There had been medical work in Cambridge for several centuries, and the Regius Professor of Physic held a chair of venerable standing. Now, however, there were enough patients available in our part of East Anglia for it to be feasible to set up a school providing full clinical training for students intending to enter the medical profession. Previously, those who had done their pre-clinical work in Cambridge had had to go on to teaching hospitals in London or elsewhere in order to complete their course. Discussions of the desirability of this new development were long and at times difficult. I felt that I perceived in myself, and in some of the others around the table, two conflicting considerations that were an influential, if unacknowledged, background. On the one hand, one had to be somewhat wary of acquiring too many medical colleagues. When it comes to competition for resources, not only is medicine expensive, but its practitioners have a tendency to proclaim that people will die if they are not immediately given all that they ask for. On the other hand, we are all getting older and the presence in the city of a first-rate medical school could have obvious advantages in the future. In the end, the Medical School was set up and it has proved to be a great success.

My service on the Council of the Senate came much later when I was President of Queens'. Four seats on the Council are reserved for occupation by Heads of Houses, a provision presumably intended to cement close relationships between the University and the Colleges. The Council's business was very varied and less focused than the concerns of the General Board. One of the most important decisions made in my time was the appointment of the University's first full-time and long-term (seven years) Vice-Chancellor (previously Heads of Houses had taken it in turn to do a two-year spell in part-time office). The choice of Sir David Williams got the new arrangement off to a good start. The Council appointed some of the members of the Financial Board, which is how I found myself in a position that was an educational experience for me, but not my natural habitat.

A committee on which I served, that was to a degree both academic and governmental in its character, was the Science Research Council (1975–9). In my last year on SRC, I was Chairman of its Nuclear Physics Board, with the task of making the case for spending the 40 million pounds or so then needed to support work in particle physics and nuclear structure for that year. This was money to be spent on fundamental physics, and its justification lay not in some claim for direct impact on national wealth, but in the intrinsic value of acquiring knowledge of the basic physical structure of the universe. An American physicist being quizzed by a Senate Committee about a very large sum of money requested for a similar kind of project in his own country, was once asked what it would do for the defence of the United States. He replied, 'Nothing, but it will help to make the United States worth defending.' It is the test of the civilized character of a prosperous country that it should devote a modest proportion of its resources to activities of intrinsically high intellectual worth.

Service on quite another kind of governmental committee started for me in an unexpected way. I was sitting in my rooms in Trinity Hall one day when my phone rang and a voice said, 'This is the Department of Health. I have the Deputy Chief Medical Officer to speak to you.' I felt that there must be some mistake, but I took the call nevertheless. Dr Abrahams explained that it was indeed me that he wanted to talk to, because a small committee was being set up to review the code of practice for the use of foetal tissue (a matter of some concern at the time, since trials were taking place of its use in treating Parkinson's disease), and they would like me to be its chairman. After meeting Dr Abrahams in Cambridge to discuss the matter, I agreed. There were just three other members of the committee: the President of the Royal College of Physicians, an eminent expert on medical law and ethics, and an experienced medical sociologist. They were all excellent colleagues and we did not find it difficult to analyse the situation and agree about what to recommend. The result was a much tighter code than that which had previously been in force. Our proposal was accepted by the Government and it still remains the guide to ethically acceptable practice in this area.

One thing leads to another. The successful completion of the work on foetal tissue led to my serving on, and sometimes chairing, a number of other governmental committees working in the general area of health and ethics. One of the most important of these was the Task Force to Review Services to Drug Misusers, of which I was the chairman. We were given two years for our work and one million pounds to spend on research related to it. Once again I found myself involved with issues of which I had had no previous experience, but I had colleagues who were very knowledgeable in the field, and we had also, in this case as in the others, the valuable assistance of civil servants and professional advisers seconded to help us. We took much evidence, both written and oral, from interested parties, visited several relevant institutions, and used the money at our disposal to set up and fund a number of research projects. The chief of these was the National Treatment Outcome Research Study (NTORS), a longitudinal study following up more than 1,000 people who, over a five-month period, had entered one of the four most commonly employed types of treatment programme. The drug scene is complex, with relapse a common feature. Nevertheless NTORS was able to demonstrate that treatment brought gains that made investment in it fully justified. In assessing achievements one had to be realistic in one's expectations. People tend not to present for drug treatment until they have hit rock bottom. It is unrealistic to expect that many will be able to make an instant transition to total abstinence. More modest gains, such as a move from injecting heroin to an oral methadone maintenance programme, represent real progress in terms of reducing health risks and enabling a more stable form of life and employment. Treatment can also significantly reduce the substantial amount of crime that frequently arises from the need to fund an addiction to illegal drugs. Our report made, in all, 79 recommendations and we believed that we had given a significant input into the formation of policy in relation to what is a major problem in society today.

My service on governmental committees also included quite a lot of work in the area of the ethical evaluation of the consequences of recent impressive developments in human genetics. For six years I was a member of the Human Genetics Advisory Commission (halfway through reconstituted with the word 'Advisory' omitted, though this did not seem to correspond to acquiring any new powers of decision). I played some part in the formation of advice to Government about policy relating to embryo research and stem cells. Personally I am happy with the cautiously permissive, case-by-case licensed and 14-day limited approach that is enshrined in current United Kingdom legislation. I have already said that there is a chapter in *Exploring Reality* which sets out in some detail the fundamental principles that I believe relate to these issues and which, in my opinion, support the UK position.

While it is not strictly speaking an ecclesiastical body, the Society for Promoting Christian Knowledge has such close connections with the churches that it can serve as my first example in that area. I served the maximum permitted period of 18 years as a member of the SPCK Governing Body. For much of that time I was chairman of its Publishing Committee. Given that I have published so many books under the SPCK imprint, this might at first sight seem to have been an inappropriately incestuous arrangement. I do not think that it was, and nor did the Charity Commissioners who had to agree publication arrangements for my books to ensure that there was no abuse of a Trustee position. The Publishing Committee's role is general accountability and oversight, and all detailed editorial decisions are rightly taken by the staff. Simon Kingston, for many years the innovative and enterprising director of publishing at SPCK and now the General Secretary of the Society, has become a good friend of mine and a shrewd and helpful commentator on my manuscripts.

During my time on the Governing Body we had two particularly difficult times of decision. One arose out of publishing and it related to a proposed book that would have contained a form of service for the blessing of same-sex unions. This would have meant a move beyond simply providing prayers that could be used by people of specific sexual orientation, for it set out liturgical provision for a ceremony that the bishops had said they would not support in the Church of England. Given the Society's close association with the Church, a number of us felt that this was something that we should not agree to publish under our imprint. For us it was not a question of censorship, but of what was appropriate for a publisher of our kind to have on its distinctive list. Arguments raged on both sides. Eventually the matter came for a final decision by the whole Governing Body. On this sensitive issue, a secret ballot was appropriate. This was conducted according to a quaint traditional practice. Each of us was given a small ball and we inserted our hands in turn into a device, within which the ball might be deposited either on the 'Yes' side or the 'No' side without the others being able to see which side had been chosen. When the balls were counted it was found that the Governing Body had decided not to proceed with the publication of the book.

The second difficult matter concerned circumstances that led to seeking the resignation of a long-serving General Secretary. This was a painful decision, but I have no doubt that it was the right one.

For the Church of England itself, its central forum is the General Synod. Cambridge University elects to Synod a Proctor in Convocation

(as clerical delegates are called), the electorate being members of the
Regent House (senior members of University or College staff) who are
in Anglican priest's orders. Similar elections in Oxford seem usually to
involve a close-run contest, but in Cambridge the recent practice has
been for a single candidate to 'emerge'. I emerged and was a Proctor for
ten years. The most significant decision taken during my time on
General Synod was to proceed with the ordination of women to the
priesthood. The debate was conducted with deep feeling on both sides,
but with great restraint and courtesy. (I had won a ticket in a ballot of
Synod members that allowed Ruth also to follow the debate from the
public gallery.) I voted for the positive decision that was reached. The
day of the debate was the only occasion on which I was absent from a
meeting of the Governing Body in Queens'. The Fellows readily recognized where my priority had to lie on this exceptional occasion. There
was great public interest in the issue, and walking up Haymarket afterwards, wearing my clerical collar, I was stopped by ticket touts hanging
around outside one of the theatres who wanted to know what the
decision had been.

Synod is a large body and so it has to conduct its debates formally,
with intending speakers being encouraged to give notice of their intentions, and with a parliamentary style of procedure. I only occasionally
spoke (in fact, only if there was a topic to which my scientific experience
seemed relevant), as I do not greatly care for that kind of formal debate.
I now think that I probably should have tried to overcome this reluc-
tance a little more than I did. What I do enjoy is sitting round a table
with a manageable number of colleagues, discussing serious issues in a
less formal way. Membership of Synod gave me this opportunity
indirectly, for it led to my becoming a member of the Church of
England's Board for Social Responsibility, and chairman of its Science,
Medicine and Technology Committee. This was work I really enjoyed.
One of the innovations we introduced at the SMT Committee was the
preparation of briefing papers on matters where both scientific and
ethical considerations had to be taken into account. The aim was to
present scientific possibilities and ethical options in an open and

even-handed way that would assist discussion at all levels in the Church, from the national to the parochial, without seeming to prescribe beforehand a specific answer. In fact, the issues involved in these matters are often so complex, and the considerations so delicately balanced, that it is not surprising that morally sensitive and responsible people may be found on both sides of the argument. Topics to which I personally contributed included genetically modified crops and embryo research.

During my first five years on the Board for Social Responsibility, its chairman was the Bishop of Liverpool, David Sheppard. I got to know him quite well and I suspect that was one reason why I came to serve for ten years as one of the Canons Theologian of Liverpool Cathedral. The distance between Liverpool and Cambridge is such that I did not manage to get to the other end more than once or twice a year, but I very much appreciated the experiences that those visits gave me. I would usually go for a long weekend, giving a talk or seminar on the Saturday and preaching in the Cathedral on the Sunday. It was stimulating to see something of life in so different and lively a civic environment. Another long-range connection I have been able to enjoy has been as one of the Six Preachers of Canterbury Cathedral. The office goes back to Reformation times, when Henry VIII was trying to make up his mind about Luther. He instructed Archbishop Cranmer to appoint six priests to travel round his diocese, three preaching for the old religion and three for the new, presumably to see what would happen and who would win. Like so many other things in English life, the office has survived while having long outlived its original purpose. We no longer career around on horseback in homiletic competition, but sporadically the Six Preachers are invited to visit Canterbury to preach in the Cathedral or to engage in some other activity of a similar kind.

17

Retirement

———➤•◄———

At the end of September 1996 I retired from being President of Queens'. Soon thereafter my successor moved into the Lodge. John Eatwell and I get on well, but I felt it only fair that I should be out of his way for a little while. As I have already mentioned, I went off to General Theological Seminary to spend a semester there as a visiting professor. The Seminary occupied a whole city block in Lower Manhattan, which had been given it by George III. (General is much older than any equivalent Anglican seminary in England, where formal theological training for ordinands only began towards the end of the nineteenth century.) Within its walls were quiet gardens and the regular worshipping life of its Chapel. Yet one could easily step out of the front door into the bustle of Ninth Avenue, to find New York's multiple resources for pleasure and culture there at one's disposal. Ruth came out for only part of my time at General, for there would not have been enough to occupy her during a long stay. While she was there we had some good times together, at the Met (both the Museum and the Opera), at concerts, and on such traditional expeditions as walking across Brooklyn Bridge and taking the Staten Island Ferry.

On my retirement I had automatically become a Fellow of Queens'. The College also kindly honoured me by making me an Honorary Fellow. (Queens' is the only College I know in which this double status is possible.) I value the continuing connection and often lunch in Queens', as well as attending grand occasions, such as the annual Smith

Feast, whose seemingly banal name belies its gastronomic splendour. Being a retired President is rather like being a grandparent – lots of fun but little responsibility.

We returned to our home in Hurst Park Avenue and joined the worshipping community of our local parish church, the Good Shepherd. The then vicar, Andrew McKearney, was very welcoming to me and most Sundays when I am at home I have had a role to play in the liturgy, either as celebrant or preacher. Ruth and I both greatly appreciated being part of ordinary parish life again, after ten years of the somewhat rarefied and episodic life of College Chapel. In population terms, the Good Shepherd is one of the largest parishes in the diocese of Ely, holding in its embrace the middle-class area that includes Hurst Park Avenue, together with a large post-war council housing estate, the Arbury. The resulting social mix makes for a varied and vigorous parish life. (We are hot stuff at jumble sales and the like.) Our size also means that we have been a training parish in which a succession of variously talented curates have served their titles.

I had been retired less than a year when, one day, I received an official brown envelope in the post. It looked like something from the Inland Revenue, but when I opened it I found it was from 10 Downing Street and it contained a largely duplicated letter informing me that the Prime Minister would like to forward my name to the Queen with the recommendation that I should be awarded the KBE (Knight Commander of the Order of the British Empire). As I remember it, below there was a tear-off strip, and I was invited to delete as appropriate in the sentence: 'It would/would not be agreeable to me to have my name put forward for the honour proposed.' One was told that nothing more would be heard from the authorities after the slip had been returned until the Honours List was published a few weeks later. I was deeply gratified to be recognized in this way and, of course, I immediately signified that I wished to accept. After I had posted the slip, I had a moment of anxiety about whether I had made the correct deletion in accordance with my intentions. Apparently I had, for my name duly appeared in the Birthday Honours.

One of the more arcane items of British protocol is that Anglican priests who are knighted do not use the prefix 'Sir'. I am inclined to suppose it to have something to do with the fact that we are not allowed to stick swords into people, though in the Middle Ages the clergy were permitted to hit people on the head with a heavy mace, provided they did not draw blood. When eventually I went to the Palace for investiture, the Queen did not tap me on the shoulder with a sword, as she usually does to knights, but simply pinned a star on my chest. I was accompanied by Ruth, together with Peter and Isobel. (Michael was in Australia, which solved what would otherwise have been a tricky family problem, as the rule is strictly three guests only.) The message about no 'Sir' has often proved difficult to get across to people, particularly in North America. Republican principles seem to coexist there with a fascination with titles. 'Yes Sir John, we quite understand,' American friends are prone to say when informed about this piece of British etiquette.

In early January 2002, I was attending a conference in Rome and staying in the Vatican City. One evening when I returned to my hotel I found a fax urging me to contact Dr Jack Templeton, the President of the John Templeton Foundation, as soon as possible. I tried to phone from my hotel room but I could not make the connection. I next tried a public phone in the hotel lobby, but was equally frustrated. Eventually I was driven to imploring the management to let me make a short call from the front desk, which they kindly did. Jack told me the splendid news that I was to be the recipient of the 2002 Templeton Prize 'for progress towards research and discovery about spiritual realities'. I was delighted and honoured to receive such a recognition, and thereby to join my scientist-theologian friends Ian Barbour and Arthur Peacocke, who were already members of the company of prizewinners. I was told that the news was to be strictly confidential until the public announcement was made in March. Of course, in my mind I exempted Ruth from this ban, but I could not face another struggle with the Italian telephone system, so that I did not tell her of my good fortune until I could do so face to face on my return home a couple of days later. We

Receiving my Templeton Prize from the Duke of Edinburgh in Buckingham Palace

both went to New York for the public announcement and the subsequent news conference and round of interviews. The actual bestowal of the Prize took place, as it always does, in May at Buckingham Palace, from the hands of the Duke of Edinburgh. I was able to tell him how pleased I was to receive the award from the Chancellor of the University of Cambridge.

The Prize is not only prestigious but it is also monetarily very valuable. In fact, it is said to be the largest money prize awarded anywhere in the world to a single individual. The sum is such that obviously one has to give most of it away in some appropriate manner. I used the greater part of my Prize to endow in perpetuity a Research Fellowship in Science and Theology at Queens' College. A year of fairly intense activity followed the award, for the Templeton Foundation quite reasonably likes to parade its latest winner. A programme of lectures at English cathedrals was organized for me, an activity which pleased me very much. One of the lectures was in Truro, where I could tell the audience not only that I had a Cornish name, but also that my grandfather had helped to build the cathedral in which we were meeting.

The last 25 years have seen a great increase in activity in the field of science and religion, and its increasing professionalization within the academy. Many books have been published and a great number of courses in the topic have come into being in colleges and universities, many encouraged by the availability of generous initial financial support from the John Templeton Foundation. My generation of workers in the field were mostly people who, after a career in science, turned in middle age to work in science and religion while continuing to earn their living by holding posts not specifically dedicated to that activity. Today young people of talent are entering the subject at the start of their academic lives by doing a PhD in science and theology. A number of permanent positions have been created at leading universities. The first of these in the United Kingdom was the Starbridge Lectureship in Theology and the Natural Sciences at Cambridge, held by my colleague Fraser Watts, who is an Anglican priest and who had a long career as a psychologist, both clinical and experimental, before turning to interdisciplinary work.

I had just discovered Susan Howatch's novels about the Church of England – which combine a strong story line with a skilful ability to portray characters who naturally talk about serious theological issues – when I read a short piece by her in a newspaper discussing her recent reading. One of the books mentioned was one of mine (I cannot now recall which one) and so I wrote to her to say that I was glad she was reading me, as I had been reading and enjoying her. A short exchange of letters followed. A few months later, I gave a lecture in London and at the dinner afterwards I unexpectedly found myself seated next to Susan. A vigorous and enjoyable conversation followed, in the course of which she told me that she would like to endow a university position in science and theology. Did I think that Cambridge would be a suitable place? I certainly did, and this soon led to her notably generous benefaction in founding the Starbridge Lectureship.

Quite soon after this, the Andreas Idreos Professorship of Science and

Religion was established at Oxford, whose first holder was the distinguished historian of science and religion, John Hedley Brooke. I also had a somewhat more distant association with this event, in that when I had been visiting CERN I had met Dr Idreos, who worked for the World Health Organization in Geneva. I had some interesting discussions with him and his wife Susan about science and religion and its academic potential, and I was able to encourage the generous plans that he already had in mind.

Much of the writing about science and religion has originated in the Christian West. Partly this is because, of all the world faith communities, Christianity is probably the one that is most concerned with intellectual issues and the pursuit of an academic approach to religious belief. 'Theology' is an indispensable word in Christian circles in a way that does not quite seem to be the case for the other faiths. Yet it is clear that those other religious traditions, including thinkers working in parts of the world outside Europe and North America, have important insights to contribute to the discussion of science and religion. To facilitate an expansion of activity, the John Templeton Foundation encouraged discussion about the possibility of founding a truly international and truly interfaith society for work in science and religion. I took part in these talks. We soon agreed that it was desirable to form a society whose members would be acknowledged experts drawn from as wide a constituency as possible, able to meet from time to time and interact with each other. Eventually this led to the founding of the International Society for Science and Religion, and I had the honour of being its first President. The inaugural meeting of the Society took place in Granada in August 2002. The venue had been chosen not only for its beauty and historic interest, but also for its appropriate associations. For a significant period in the later Middle Ages, southern Spain had been a place where fruitful intellectual exchange had taken place between adherents of the three Abrahamic faiths, an exchange sadly brought to an end when the Christians began to harass and expel their Jewish and Islamic neighbours. Granada is also close to the border between Africa and Europe and so it symbolized something of the geographical scope of our ambitions for the new Society. ISSR successfully got under way and it has continued to grow and flourish under my successors in the Presidency.

As has been the experience of so many other people, retirement has been a pretty active time for me. I don't want simply to sit in a rocking chair all day, and so I can't complain. After all, I only do what I have agreed to do. With writing and speaking, church duties and some gardening, I manage to keep out of mischief.

After I had been retired about six years, Ruth went one day to see our GP about some problems she had been having with her eyesight. They were recognized as being due to the anomalous thickness of her blood and she was referred to the Haematology Department at Addenbrookes Hospital. This led to the diagnosis of Waldenstrom's macroglobulinaemia, a comparatively rare form of leukaemia. Initial chemotherapy proved very effective and Ruth enjoyed more than two years of remission, during which we were able to continue travelling abroad quite frequently, including visits to Australia and China. However, the disease then recurred and the further therapeutic strategies that were tried ultimately did not prove successful. Gradually Ruth's condition deteriorated until she was being maintained by fortnightly transfusions, permitting only a limited degree of activity at home. Eventually, an emergency admission following an acute infection saw her back in Addenbrookes for the last fortnight of her life. For about ten days Ruth was sufficiently aware to be able to enjoy short visits from her children and some close friends. The last of these visits was on Mothering Sunday 2006, when she was able to give our grand-daughter Elizabeth a violin that she had been making for her at the Cambridge Violin Workshop, the centre for amateur stringed-instrument making where Ruth had earlier made herself a cello. This day was also our 51st wedding anniversary and it was a very happy and important occasion for Ruth and for all of us. The next day a very noticeable deterioration began in her condition and she started to sink into bouts of unconsciousness. Ruth died peacefully on the

Wednesday, with her children and myself at her bedside. Throughout the more than four years of her long struggle with Waldenstrom's, Ruth had shown great courage and determination, sustained by her strong Christian faith. Her funeral at the Good Shepherd took place on the Tuesday of Holy Week. It was an occasion of thankfulness and hope. The large congregation, and the many kind and appreciative letters that we received, were a great source of consolation to all her family. It was fittingly symbolic that the single display of white flowers that had stood beside her coffin at her funeral, returned to our church a few days later to be part of the flowers for Easter. For the Christian, death is real, and it brings about a real separation from a much-loved companion, but it is not the ultimate reality, for that is the eternal faithfulness of God.

No one knows when or how their own life will end, but we all know that death is ahead of us sometime. For a long while I have prayed regularly that I may be given the grace to make a good death. For the Christian, it will be the final act in this world of complete commitment into the hands of a faithful God and merciful Saviour. I greatly value the words of a Charles Wesley hymn that for me express perfectly how one should seek to think about one's death,

> Ready for all thy perfect will,
>   My acts of faith and love repeat,
> Till death thine endless mercies seal,
>   And make the sacrifice complete.

With Ruth by Queens' Chapel

Bibliography

Books by J. C. Polkinghorne

1966 *The Analytic S-Matrix* (Cambridge University Press); with R. J. Eden, P. V. Landshoff and D. I. Olive.

1979 *The Particle Play* (W. H. Freeman).

1980 *Models of High Energy Processes* (Cambridge University Press).

1983 *The Way the World Is* (Triangle/Eerdmans, 1984).

1984 *The Quantum World* (Longman/Princeton University Press, 1985; Penguin, 1986).

1986 *One World* (SPCK/Princeton University Press, 1987; Templeton Foundation Press, 2007).

1988 *Science and Creation* (SPCK/New Science Library, 1989; Templeton Foundation Press, 2006).

1989 *Science and Providence* (SPCK/New Science Library; Templeton Foundation Press, 2005).

1991 *Reason and Reality* (SPCK/Trinity Press International).

1994 *Science and Christian Belief* (SPCK); also published as *The Faith of a Physicist* (Princeton University Press, 1994; Fortress, 1996).

1994   *Quarks, Chaos and Christianity* (Triangle/Crossroad, 1996; second edition: SPCK/Crossroad, 2005).

1995   *Serious Talk* (Trinity Press International/SCM Press, 1996).

1996   *Scientists as Theologians* (SPCK).

1996   *Beyond Science* (Cambridge University Press).

1996   *Searching for Truth* (Bible Reading Fellowship/Crossroad).

1998   *Belief in God in an Age of Science* (Yale University Press).

1998   *Science and Theology* (SPCK/Fortress).

2000   *The End of the World and the Ends of God* (Trinity Press International); edited with Michael Welker.

2000   *Traffic in Truth* (Canterbury Press/Fortress).

2000   *Faith, Science and Understanding* (SPCK/Yale University Press).

2001   *The Work of Love* (SPCK/Eerdmans); editor.

2001   *Faith in the Living God* (SPCK/Fortress); with Michael Welker.

2002   *The God of Hope and the End of the World* (SPCK/Yale University Press).

2002   *Quantum Theory: A very short introduction* (Oxford University Press).

2003   *The Archbishop's School of Christianity and Science* (York Courses).

2003   *Living with Hope* (SPCK/Westminster John Knox).

2004   *Science and the Trinity* (SPCK/Yale University Press).

2005   *Exploring Reality* (SPCK/Yale University Press).

2007   *Quantum Physics and Theology* (SPCK/Yale University Press).

Index